*Diseases and Disorders*

# Autism

Titles in the Diseases and Disorders series include:

Alzheimer's Disease
Attention Deficit Disorder
Down Syndrome
Epilepsy
Learning Disabilities
Phobias

# Autism

### by Michele Engel Edwards

Library of Congress Cataloging-in-Publication Data

Edwards, Michele Engel.
   Autism / by Michele Engel Edwards.
      p. cm. — (Diseases and disorders)
Includes bibliographical references and index.
   ISBN 156006-829-9
   1. Autism—Juvenile literature. 2. Autism in children—
Juvenile literature. [1. Autism. 2. Mentally handicapped.] I.
Title. II. Diseases and disorders series.
RC553.A88 E39 2001
616.89'82—dc21

                              00-011221

# *Table of Contents*

# "The Most Difficult Puzzles Ever Devised"

Cᴴᴬᴿᴸᴱˢ Bᴱˢᵀ, ᴼɴᴱ of the pioneers in the search for a cure for diabetes, once explained what it is about medical research that intrigued him so. "It's not just the gratification of knowing one is helping people," he confided, "although that probably is a more heroic and selfless motivation. Those feelings may enter in, but truly, what I find best is the feeling of going toe to toe with nature, of trying to solve the most difficult puzzles ever devised. The answers are there somewhere, those keys that will solve the puzzle and make the patient well. But how will those keys be found?"

Since the dawn of civilization, nothing has so puzzled people—and often frightened them, as well—as the onset of illness in a body or mind that had seemed healthy before. A seizure, the inability of a heart to pump, the sudden deterioration of muscle tone in a small child—being unable to reverse such conditions or even to understand why they occur was unspeakably frustrating to healers. Even before there were names for such conditions, even before they were understood at all, each was a reminder of how complex the human body was, and how vulnerable.

While our grappling with understanding diseases has been frustrating at times, it has also provided some of humankind's most heroic accomplishments. Alexander Fleming's accidental discovery in 1928 of a mold that could be turned into penicillin

6

has resulted in the saving of untold millions of lives. The isolation of the enzyme insulin has reversed what was once a death sentence for anyone with diabetes. There have been great strides in combating conditions for which there is not yet a cure, too. Medicines can help AIDS patients live longer, diagnostic tools such as mammography and ultrasounds can help doctors find tumors while they are treatable, and laser surgery techniques have made the most intricate, minute operations routine.

This "toe-to-toe" competition with diseases and disorders is even more remarkable when seen in a historical continuum. An astonishing amount of progress has been made in a very short time. Just two hundred years ago, the existence of germs as a cause of some diseases was unknown. In fact, it was less than 150 years ago that a British surgeon named Joseph Lister had difficulty persuading his fellow doctors that washing their hands before delivering a baby might increase the chances of a healthy delivery (especially if they had just attended to a diseased patient)!

Each book in Lucent's *Diseases and Disorders* series explores a disease or disorder and the knowledge that has been accumulated (or discarded) by doctors through the years. Each book also examines the tools used for pinpointing a diagnosis, as well as the various means that are used to treat or cure a disease. Finally, new ideas are presented—techniques or medicines that may be on the horizon.

Frustration and disappointment are still part of medicine, for not every disease or condition can be cured or prevented. But the limitations of knowledge are being pushed outward constantly; the "most difficult puzzles ever devised" are finding challengers every day.

# Introduction

U P UNTIL SIXTY years ago, even scientists referred to those afflicted with autism as "idiots," "imbeciles," and "cretins," and some thought autistic individuals were insane. Then two scientists working with mentally disturbed children in the 1940s recognized that one group of children shared certain types of behaviors that set them apart from the rest. Sometimes retarded, but definitely not insane, these children overwhelmingly showed an inability to form relationships with others.

It was at this time that the label "autism," meaning a kind of aloneness, was applied to those whose behavior fit the newly developed diagnosis. Unable to discover a single cause of the disorder, one famous psychiatrist promoted a theory that became

*A woman spends time with her autistic son, who was erroneously treated for mental illness many years before he was correctly diagnosed.*

popular for many years—that autism was caused by "refrigerator mothers," women who rejected their children and caused them to withdraw from the world. Scientists now know that autism is a medical disorder and have found some clues to its origins, but many mysteries remain. Until they are solved, there will be no cure, but some treatments do exist to help manage some of autism's symptoms.

Though numerous children with autism make great strides if they are diagnosed early enough and are able to find the right medical treatment and educational support, most will never marry, have a job, or live independently. Half of all autistic children will never learn to speak. Those autistics suffering from a less severe form of the disorder, called Asperger's syndrome, have a brighter future to look forward to, as described by well-known author Oliver Sacks:

> The word "autism" still conveys a fixed and dreadful meaning to most people—they visualize a child mute, rocking, screaming, inaccessible, cut off from human contact. . . . These pictures are not wholly false, but they fail to indicate that there are forms of autism which (while they may indeed go with ways of thinking and perceiving very different from the "normal") do not incapacitate in the same way, but may (especially if there is high intelligence, and understanding, and education) allow lives that are full of event and achievement, and a special sort of insight and courage, too."[1]

According to recent studies, as many as two of every thousand children born today will be diagnosed with autism. The disorder affects a half million children and adults in the United States, and it is four to five times more likely to affect boys than girls. Girls with the disorder, however, tend to have more severe symptoms and lower intelligence. The chance of autism occurring in a family is not affected by such factors as income, race, ethnicity, lifestyle, or educational background. Autism is the third most common developmental disorder after mental retardation and cerebral palsy, and it is more common than childhood cancer, diabetes, or Down syndrome.

*Teachers assist students at a school for autistic children in Utah. Special schools and programs for people with autism are helping to improve the quality of life for people with the disorder.*

Despite the fact that it is so common, the public—including many professionals in the medical, educational, and vocational fields—are still unaware of how autism affects people and how they can effectively work with individuals with autism. Only over the last decade has real progress been made in understanding the disorder. No longer are autistic children shunted off to live in institutions that are too large and impersonal to meet their individual needs. They receive special education through public or private schools, and additional services exist in the community to assist those who want to pursue college, employment, and independent living. The quality of their lives will continue to improve as more about this baffling disorder is understood.

# Chapter 1

# What Is Autism?

THE EXACT NATURE of autism is still a mystery. It wasn't until 1943 that Leo Kanner, a scientist at Johns Hopkins University, identified a condition he called "early infantile autism." He had studied the behavior of eleven children who had been diagnosed with schizophrenia, a severe mental disorder. Kanner noted that although these eleven children's cases closely resembled one another, they were strikingly different from those of the other schizophrenic children, as he explains:

> Since 1938, there have come to our attention a number of children whose condition differs so markedly and uniquely from anything reported so far, that each case merits—and, I hope, will eventually receive—a detailed consideration of its fascinating peculiarities.[2]

Dr. Kanner noted that unlike the schizophrenic children, the autistic children did not tend to have a family history of mental illness, did not eventually experience hallucinations, and showed signs of their disorder in very early childhood. He emphasized three features that distinguished autistic children from schizophrenic children: social isolation, insistence on sameness, and abnormal language. Kanner noted that the primary feature of the disability was that of social withdrawal, so he named it "autism," which he defined as being immersed within oneself: "There is from the start an extreme autistic aloneness that, whenever possible, disregards, ignores, shuts out anything that comes to the child from the outside."[3]

*First paragraph Introduction*

## A Disorder, but Not a Disease

In the years since Kanner identified autism, experts have yet to find just one set of physical symptoms that defines the condition,

11

*The primary feature of autism is social withdrawal. Autistic children typically become isolated and attempt to shut out the outside world.*

which means they cannot classify it as a disease. There is no fever, swelling, or visible sign of the disorder. People with autism look just like people who are not autistic. Doctors can use standard medical tests to diagnose illnesses and diseases such as allergies, infections, pneumonia, heart disease, diabetes, and cancer, but a blood test will not indicate the presence of autism, nor will an X ray, a urinalysis (a set of chemical tests conducted on a urine sample), or a biopsy (a set of laboratory tests conducted on a sample of human tissue). So doctors rely exclusively on behavior to determine whether a child is autistic.

Based on what they know about how the brain functions in nondisabled people, experts at the National Institute of Mental Health (NIMH) describe autism as a

brain disorder that typically affects a person's ability to communicate, form relationships with others, and respond appropriately to the environment. Some people with autism are relatively high-functioning, with speech and intelligence intact. Others are mentally retarded, mute, or have serious language delays. For some, autism makes them seem closed off and shut down, others seem locked into repetitive behaviors (self-stimulation) and rigid patterns of thinking.[4]

Although autism is clearly a mental disorder, scientists have determined that it is not the same thing as depression, anxiety, addiction, mental retardation, or other mental conditions—although someone who is autistic may also be depressed or anxious, addicted to alcohol or drugs, or mentally retarded. For the time being, medical experts have classified autism under the heading "pervasive developmental disorder" (PDD)—which the American Psychiatric Association defines as "a general category of disorders which are characterized by severe and pervasive impairment in several areas of development."[5]

## Early Clues

A diagnosis of autism is almost always made within the first three to four years of a child's life, when parents notice that their son or daughter is developing differently than other children. Normally infants behave in ways that demonstrate they need and want contact with other human beings. Early on, they look around at people, turn toward voices, grasp and hold on to a finger, and smile at those around them. Within the first three months, they recognize and smile at the sound of their mother's voice and soon reach for her with their hands. They babble and learn simple words like "mama" and "dada." By about the end of their first year, they point to objects to get others to pay attention to the same thing, and—perhaps as an early sign of their ability to show empathy for another human being—they will mirror a look of sadness on someone else's face.

Some autistic children never reach these stages; others may pass through them at a later age. Autistic children avoid eye contact and may shrink away from touch instead of wanting to be cuddled. They may stiffen or go limp when picked up and will not cling happily to a parent who has returned after an absence.

*Non-autistic children interact in ways that demonstrate their desire for human contact. In contrast, autistic children often avoid eye contact and shrink away from touch.*

They may not even be able to tell the difference between their parents and strangers.

Parents usually know by age two or three that something is wrong. Although the parents may be tempted to ignore the symptoms, hoping that their child is just going through a stage, eventually the child's behavior either worsens or simply continues for so long that the parents feel they must consult a specialist to determine the cause and to seek treatment.

## Diagnosis

It is then that autism is diagnosed by observing the child's behavior, communication skills, and social interactions. Medical tests are completed to rule out other possible causes of autistic symptoms. Children who are autistic display some or all of a number of behaviors: they do not understand how to play "hide-and-seek," "Mother May I," or games that require the ability to pretend. They are not able to make friends with other children the same age and do not begin and sustain conversations with others. They use language in unusual ways, repeating certain phrases over and over again or suddenly blurting out a comment that makes no sense within the context of the situation. They are interested in just a few activities, and their interest in those activities is unusually intense. They are inflexible about daily routines and rituals, insisting that things be done precisely the same way every time. And they are preoccupied with parts of objects rather than comprehending objects and their function as a whole.

Medical practitioners, usually psychologists, begin the diagnostic process by having the child complete a series of standardized tests that provide information about the child's vocabulary and language skills, intelligence, social maturity, and emotional adjustment. However, these tests lose their value if the child also suffers from severe psychological problems that prevent him or her from participating fully in the assessment process. During the process of diagnosing the disorder, experts also determine whether the individual shows signs of being afflicted with other disorders as well.

## Related Disorders

Autism is a complex disorder and one that is sometimes accompanied by other nervous system disorders. About one-third of autistic children experience seizures, which range from brief periods during which they lose consciousness, called blackouts, to full-blown body convulsions. A diagnostic test called an electroencephalogram (EEG) can confirm the presence of seizures, and there are medications that can control them.

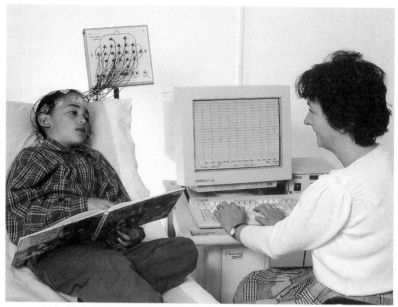

*Approximately one-third of autistic children experience seizures, the presence of which can be confirmed by performing an electroencephalogram (EEG).*

Another disorder that sometimes accompanies autism is called the Fragile X syndrome, and it appears in about 10 percent of cases, mostly in males. It is an inherited disorder that is named for a defective piece of the X chromosome. The X chromosome, which is attached to the body's set of chemical instructions called DNA, is the organic structure that carries the information that determines individual hereditary characteristics. Fragile X is diagnosed if the X chromosome appears pinched and fragile under a microscope. Those born with this disorder have many of the same symptoms of autism, along with mental retardation and unusual physical features that are not typical of autism.

Also related to autism is a condition called tuberous sclerosis, a rare genetic disorder that causes abnormal tissue growth in the brain and problems in other organs. It occurs less than once in ten thousand births, and about a quarter of those born with the condition are also autistic.

Most autistic children, about 70 percent, are considered mentally retarded, scoring below average on intelligence tests. About

20 percent have normal intelligence, and about 10 percent score higher than average. However, it is difficult to test the intelligence of autistic children because of their communication problems. They may actually know the answers to the questions but are unable to communicate the answers in a way that the people administering the test can understand. Therefore, many experts believe that mental retardation and autism are separate conditions that may coexist in the same child.

In rare cases, autistic individuals possess remarkable abilities in areas such as math, music, or drawing. Researchers at the National Institute of Mental Health report:

> At a young age, when other children are drawing straight lines and scribbling, some children with autism are able to draw detailed, realistic pictures in three-dimensional perspective. Some toddlers who are autistic are so visually skilled that they can put complex jigsaw puzzles together. Many begin to read exceptionally early—sometimes even before they begin to speak. Some who have a keenly developed sense of hearing can play musical instruments they have never been taught, play a song accurately after hearing it once, or name any note they hear.[6]

Such individuals are sometimes called "idiot savants," meaning a mentally defective person with an exceptional skill or talent in a special field.

## Tests, Interviews, Observations, and Checklists

Because autism is such a complex disorder, those who diagnose it rely heavily on information provided by parents, teachers, and informal observations of the child. They ask questions about the child's developmental history, including the ages at which the child could sit unassisted and began walking. They examine social behavior, finding out whether the child makes eye contact with people or shows affection. They document whether the child speaks at all and, if so, how well. They observe the child's emotional state, noting whether the child has irrational or inappropriate fears or mood swings that seem to have no cause. They also seek out information about behavior problems, asking observers whether the child is toilet trained and able to eat and dress without assistance, throws tantrums, or in any way exhibits aggressive behavior.

This input from parents and others is crucial; however, it is also important for practitioners to observe the child in a struc-

*Before an accurate diagnosis of autism can be made, a child's behavior and interaction with parents and teachers is carefully examined.*

tured setting to confirm the information received from others and to determine how the child responds in a different setting and with an unfamiliar person. The clinician notes whether the child will make eye contact (either spontaneously or by request), how the child interacts with toys, the level of speech the child has mastered, whether the child engages in appropriate behaviors, and how the child interacts with his or her parents.

In addition to standardized tests, interviews, and observation sessions, clinicians use one of a number of evaluation checklists. Typically, these tools are most helpful during the initial screening process. An important advantage of using them is that each child is assessed using the same criteria.

Medical testing, standardized tests, interviews, observations, and checklists reveal important information that may result in a diagnosis of autism. However, as one specialist points out,

> just knowing that a child has a diagnosis of autism does not provide sufficient information about the behavioral characteristics and needs of that particular child. For example, one child may have fairly sophisticated language skills, minimal self-stimulation, and some appropriate play. Another child may be completely nonverbal, have pervasive self-stimulation, and no play skills. Despite quite different behavioral repertoires, both these children are labeled autistic.[7]

Therefore, researchers must look carefully at an autistic child's behavior in order to find out which subgroup of autism the child might fit into and to describe in as clear a way as possible each child's unique symptoms. "Although people with autism do not have exactly the same symptoms and deficits, they tend to share certain social, communication, motor, and sensory problems that affect their behavior in predictable ways,"[8] says a specialist at the National Institute of Mental Health. The most common signs of autism are easy to recognize.

## Sensory and Motor Problems

Faulty perception is usually the first sign of autism. An expert at the National Institute of Mental Health explains:

*Although these autistic children share certain social and communication problems that are typical of the disorder, their behavioral characteristics and needs are likely to vary widely.*

When children's perceptions are accurate, they can learn from what they see, feel, or hear. On the other hand, if sensory information is faulty or if the input from the various senses fails to merge into a coherent picture, the child's experiences of the world can be confusing. People with autism seem to have one or both of these problems. There may be problems in the sensory signals that reach the brain or in the integration of the sensory signals—and quite possibly both.[9]

Some autistics are painfully sensitive to certain sounds, textures, tastes, and smells. A child may not be able to tolerate wearing anything but clothes made of pure cotton. A gentle hug may overwhelm another child. Some cover their ears at the sound of a vacuum cleaner, a telephone, a distant airplane, or even the wind—as if the decibel level was extremely high. Strangely, some autistics do not react to extreme cold or pain. A child with autism may fall and break a bone and never cry. Another may hit his or her head against a hard surface without wincing. And some autistics receive scrambled sensory messages. One individual may hear a sound when his or her elbow is touched; another may experience certain sounds as colors. Many autistics also exhibit awkwardness in doing fine work with their fingers and handling small objects. Their physical coordination is often impaired, which makes it difficult for them to walk, run, and climb normally.

To the outside observer, the autistic individual seems to be out of touch with reality, reacting to normal events in baffling ways. Temple Grandin, who is autistic and has written a book about her experiences, provides insight into the unique sensory problems that created a chaotic world for her:

> Reality to an autistic person is a confusing interacting mass of events, people, places, sounds and sights. There seem to be no clear boundaries, order or meaning to anything. A large part of my life is spent just trying to work out the pattern behind everything.[10]

## Repetitive Behaviors and Obsessions

Another common sign of autism is the presence of repetitive behaviors and obsessions. It may be that repetitive behavior serves to block out painful sensations for autistics. Order and sameness may provide a sense of safety in a world of sensory confusion. Despite the fact that children with autism may display a normal appearance and good muscle control, their odd repetitive motions set them apart from nonautistic children. Rocking back and forth, hand flapping, and hair twirling are common. One child might walk on tiptoe; another might freeze in position. According to the National Institute of Mental Health, "Experts call such behaviors *stereotypies* or *self-stimulation.*"[11]

Repetitive actions, like spending hours lining up pretzel sticks or loading and unloading batteries in a flashlight, occur frequently. Autistics may become fixated on specific objects—like one girl who was so obsessed with digital watches that she would grab the arms of strangers to look at their wrists.

Autistic persons lack a sense of imagination and have an intense need for constancy. They won't engage in make-believe

*An autistic man is engrossed in watching and playing with a small object. Repetitive behaviors and obsessions are common signs of autism.*

play, and games like peekaboo and patty-cake are impossible for them to understand. They may pick one object or subject to focus on and ignore all others, and they find it difficult to shift or divide their attention. Requesting that they move from one activity to another can upset them tremendously. Everywhere in their lives they impose rigid routines, and they may panic if, for example, the furniture in their living room has been rearranged. They frequently want to wear the same clothes every day, take the same routes every time they go anywhere, and follow the same schedules.

## Language Problems

Another distinctive characteristic of people with autism is their limited ability to speak. Nearly half of autistic children remain mute throughout their lives. Others use language that is unintelligible. Many cannot hold a conversation or understand simple questions.

Nondisabled infants coo and babble during the first six months and will say words by the age of one. They respond to hearing their name, point when they want something, and say no when offered something distasteful. By the age of two, they can follow simple directions and put together short sentences like "more cookie."

Infants who are autistic may also coo and babble at first, but they soon stop. Some learn to speak much later, as late as age eight in some cases. Others may use sign language or eventually have to learn to communicate using special electronic equipment.

Autistic children who do learn to speak often rely exclusively on single words to communicate. They typically confuse the pronouns "I," "my," and "you," which change meaning depending on who is speaking. When a teacher asks an autistic child named Tom, "What is my name?" the child is likely to answer, "My name is Tom."

An autistic child may only be able to parrot what he or she hears, a condition known as echolalia. The child may repeat a question someone asked or an advertisement on the radio. Or the child may suddenly shout something like, "Throw it away," a phrase the child heard a parent say weeks before.

Some autistic children repeat the same phrase in a variety of different situations. Though this may seem bizarre at first, there is usually a meaningful pattern behind it. For example, a child may say "Get in the car" at random times throughout the day. The child may associate getting in the car with leaving the house, and so uses that phrase to indicate wanting to go outdoors. Or a child may say "milk and cookies" when pleased because of the association between good feelings about this treat and good feelings about the current cause of pleasure.

Understanding the body language of a person with autism can be difficult. For most nonautistic people, there is a relationship between facial expressions or gestures and what is being communicated in words. They smile when talking about things they enjoy or shrug when they can't answer a question. By contrast, facial expressions, movements, and gestures rarely match what an autistic child is saying. Even their tone of voice fails to reflect their feelings; they commonly speak in a high-pitched, singsong, or flat robotlike voice.

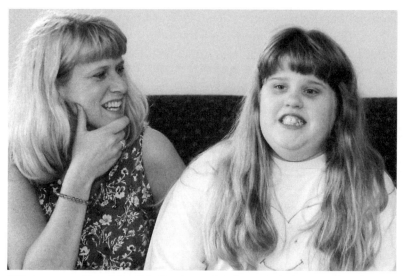

*This ten-year-old autistic girl attends special classes to help strengthen her communication skills. Limited language ability makes it difficult for people with autism to communicate their thoughts and needs.*

## Social Problems

Impaired social interaction is the hallmark feature of autism. Children with autism avoid looking at other people and may fail to respond to their own names. Facial expressions and tone of voice hold no meaning for such children, so they are unable to interpret others' emotions or cues about appropriate behavior. An autistic child will think the meaning is the same whether the mother says "Come here" while smiling and extending her arms for a hug or while squinting and planting her fists on her hips.

Most five-year-olds have learned to see things from another person's perspective, but autistic children may never learn this. They don't understand that others have different information, feelings, and goals than they have; and this inability makes it impossible for them to predict or understand another's actions. An example of this is demonstrated by a study in which

> researchers quizzed children about a scenario in which a girl named Sally places a marble in a covered basket and leaves the

room. While Sally is out, her friend Anne moves the marble from the basket into a nearby covered box. When asked where Sally would later look for her marble, even retarded children knew she would expect to find it where she'd left it. By contrast, most autistic children thought she would look in the box. They couldn't see the world through Sally's eyes.[12]

Aggressive physical behavior makes social relationships still more difficult. Autistics tend to lose control, especially when angry, frustrated, or faced with a strange or overwhelming environment. They react by breaking things, attacking others, or harming themselves. Some will bang their heads against a wall, pull their hair, bite their arms, or engage in other self-destructive behavior.

## Growing Up with Autism

Once a child has been diagnosed as autistic because he or she exhibits some or all of the disorder's characteristics, some practitioners try to avoid telling parents, who they fear may lose hope upon hearing the word "autism." Instead, those practitioners simply describe the child as having a severe communication disorder or nervous system disorder. And children with mild or fewer symptoms are often diagnosed as having pervasive developmental disorder (PDD), which is so general that it seems less challenging to parents. Most practitioners, however, feel comfortable using the label *autistic* and urge parents to obtain access to the full range of treatment measures and services available to autistic children.

Often, in fact, the symptoms of autism do change over time, improving with medication, modifications to diet, specialized training in language and social skills, and other interventions—and as the children mature. Some adolescents with autism go through a period of depression, and behavior problems may worsen at that time. With the proper information, parents and teachers can often adjust to meet the changing needs of the child.

It is possible for some people with autism to lead normal or nearly normal lives. Indeed, here is one mother's account of a typical day in the life of her twenty-three-year-old autistic daughter:

Jessy's day begins early. She rises as punctually for work as she did for school. She has laid out her clothes—colors carefully harmonized—the night before, so as to have plenty of time to shower, make her bed, and eat a leisurely breakfast, for she becomes anxious if she thinks she's going to be late. She has an alarm clock, but she doesn't need it. Her father or I may have breakfast with her, but it's for sociability, not supervision. She will leave the house on the dot, whether or not we're there. She returns from her job in mid-afternoon; at home she will occupy herself dusting and vacuuming, doing the laundry, ironing. She mends her clothes, on the machine or by hand. She weaves on the loom she bought with her own earnings, setting up the warp herself, not merely throwing the shuttle. She can put in a new washer when the faucet drips. At the sight of this cheerful, useful member of our household, the long, inert years might almost be forgotten.[13]

Jessy's story, and others like it, is a source of hope to many parents of autistic children.

# Chapter 2

# Possible Causes and Treatments

SCIENTISTS DO NOT know what causes autism. After more than fifty years of research, there are many theories but no single, satisfying answer. Scientists have looked for possible causes in four primary areas. First they studied how autistic children and their parents related to one another. They looked at whether the parents of autistic children treat their children differently than do the parents of children without autism. Then they tried to understand the role that genetics might play in causing autism. They wondered whether autism might be an inherited disorder. They also investigated the size and function of the autistic's brain, comparing it to the brain of a nonautistic person. In addition, scientists tried to determine whether an autistic's immune system works differently. The results of these studies have led some scientists to believe that there may be more than one cause.

Until a single cause or a set of causes is known, autism cannot be cured. In the meantime, much of what scientists have learned in the process of understanding the disorder's possible causes has led to the discovery of effective treatments for some of its symptoms.

## Social Environment

At the time that autism was first identified, many doctors generally believed that if they could not find a disorder's physical cause, then it must be caused by the social environment created by the child's parents in the home. Dr. Kanner, who was the first

*Doctor Bruno Bettelheim believed that children who became autistic were unusually sensitive and reacted to cold, unresponsive parents by purposely withdrawing.*

to work with autistic children and their parents, suggested that these parents were different in some ways from the parents of other children. He described them as "cold, detached, aloof, . . . and lacking in emotional warmth," and he coined the term "refrigerator parents" to describe their personalities.[14] He never stated that the parents were the sole cause of the disease, but he suspected that autistic children may have been born with a tendency to withdraw socially and that their parents' behavior triggered the disease.

Another famous doctor, Bruno Bettelheim, had a more direct explanation of the parents' role in fostering autism. He believed that children who become autistic are unusually sensitive to their experiences. If the parents of these children behaved in an abnormally cold manner, he reported, then the children reacted by withdrawing from the environment and becoming less responsive to their parents. He concluded that "children who become autistic have parents who are either unwilling or unable to provide satisfactory responses to their child, and withdrawal is a willful act on the part of the children."[15] Because of these scientists' beliefs, doctors urged the parents of many autistic children to place them in special institutions so that they could live with other disabled children and be cared for by adults trained to help them with their unique problems.

The idea that parents were the cause of their child's autism persisted from 1943 until the 1960s, but new information about the relationships between parents and their autistic children has led scientists to believe that the early theories were incorrect.

*Thankfully for the many parents of autistic children, including this woman who has two kids with autism, theories that blamed the disorder on parents have largely been rejected.*

Many studies have shown that those theories were based on information that may not have been true or reliable. There is no strong proof that all parents of autistic children behave abnormally toward their child. In fact, in 1978 a major study "demonstrated that parents of autistic children do not differ from parents of normal children . . . in the areas of personality and social interaction."[16] Once scientists rejected the theory that parents were responsible for autism in their children, they began to look at the role genetics might play in causing the disorder.

## Genetics

Biologists study how living things come to be, how they grow, and how they behave. They know that a substance called DNA (deoxyribonucleic acid) contains cells called genes, which contain a set of instructions that each human being is born with and that determines his or her personal traits. Such traits include the individual's physical appearance, including height, eye color, hair color, skin color, and other features; intelligence level; special abilities; and the likelihood of suffering from certain diseases and health problems.

DNA is passed down from grandparents to parents to child, and the instructions change a little bit each time. So a person who is tall, has brown eyes, and is athletic probably inherited those traits from a parent, grandparent, or great-grandparent who also had one or more of those traits. Each person's DNA is almost the same as everyone else's, but each person's is also just different enough from anyone else's to make each individual unique (except in the case of identical twins).

When scientists studied people with autism, one of the first things they noticed was that many autistic children also have an autistic brother or sister. A family that has one child with autism has a greater chance of having another autistic child than a family without any autistic children. Therefore, the disorder may be hereditary, carried in the genetic structure passed on through the family. In one study, researchers looked at a hundred families that had two children with autism. They compared the parents' and the children's DNA by taking blood samples and examining them under a microscope. They discovered that two of the autistic children's chromosomes, which are the cells that carry the genetic information, were defective. They were either malformed or broken, and such damage is usually the cause of certain diseases and disorders. One scientist concluded, "The data is pretty overwhelming that autism is strongly genetic. We believe there must be more than one gene involved in autism."[17]

## Size and Functioning of the Brain

Some of the same scientists who are looking at the role of genetics in causing autism are also looking at the size and function of the brain for clues to understanding the causes of the disorder. Studies have shown that the brain of someone with autism is larger than the brain of a nonautistic person and that certain areas of the brain responsible for memory and emotional functioning contain abnormally small cells.

Researchers have also found abnormally low blood circulation in some parts of the brain that are responsible for intellectual

*Families like this, in which all three sons are autistic, support theories that the disorder is strongly genetic.*

functioning. Smaller cells carry less information and low blood circulation carries less oxygen to those parts of the brain, which may be why they do not function as well as they should. Scientists don't yet know enough about how each part of the brain actually works to understand exactly how these abnormalities affect the behavior of autistics.

## The Immune System

Other clues about what causes autism are found in the immune system, whose cells play a key role in the way the body protects itself against the germs that cause disease and disorders. When germs, in the form of bacteria or viruses, try to invade the body, the immune system recognizes that they don't belong to the body and responds by producing cells called antibodies to fight them off. Anything that causes the system to respond like this is called an antigen. An antigen can be fairly harmless, such as grass pollen, or harmful, such as a flu virus. In humans, the immune system starts to develop in the embryo and is fully formed by the time a baby is born.

Scientists believe that people with autism may have weaker or more sensitive immune systems than normal. They noticed that autistics are more likely than others to suffer from certain autoimmune diseases, such as rheumatoid arthritis, which causes pain, stiffness, swelling, deformity, and loss of function in the joints. Autoimmune diseases occur when the immune system's antibodies act as if the body's own tissue is foreign and attacks it while fighting off the antigen.

Researchers also found that the blood of autistic children who had been exposed to certain viruses contained too many of the antibodies that are assigned to work on brain cells. People with autism may have immune systems that overreact to a virus by attacking and actually damaging the individual's own brain cells.

Using what they know about how the immune system works, scientists have found ways to prevent some harmful diseases, like the measles and the mumps, by giving people vaccinations against them at an early age. A vaccination, taken orally or by injection, works by giving the person a small, very mild form of the virus that causes a disease—just enough to teach the antibodies what to look for and how to fight it off in the future if necessary. This strengthens the body's ability to resist those antigens by allowing it to practice defending itself. Some children experience mild side effects in response to vaccines, but most do not.

Some parents of autistic children have grown concerned, however, that their child's vaccinations may have caused autism. One parent reported that his son

> was born a normal, healthy child. At seven months, he received his third of four vaccination shots. Within 72 hours, he developed a high fever and shrieked with a high, wailing scream for days. He began losing eye contact, smiling less, losing interest in people and had constant croup and was

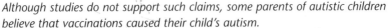

*Although studies do not support such claims, some parents of autistic children believe that vaccinations caused their child's autism.*

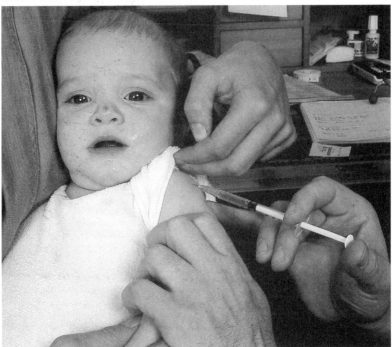

chronically ill. At 18 months, he received his first mumps, measles and rubella vaccination. Within days he lost most of his remaining skills, developing severe sleep irregularities, chronic gastrointestinal problems and expressing constant pain exhibited by harrowing days of endless crying. At 2-and-a-half years old, he was officially diagnosed with autism.[18]

Reports like this one have caused many parents and some scientists to wonder whether vaccines are as safe as they once thought. Most scientists claim that the dangers of vaccination are not that great, and they worry that if parents stop vaccinating their children, many serious diseases like polio that have nearly been eradicated may again take their toll. In an effort to reassure parents, researchers examined information about 498 children with autism born since 1979, which is when doctors began giving the mumps, measles, and rubella vaccine to children under two years old. When they compared the group of children that had been vaccinated to the group that had not, they found that the same number of children who had not been vaccinated were diagnosed with autism at the same age as those who had. Therefore, they concluded, it is unlikely that their autism was caused by the vaccination.

Another reason that scientists believe that autism is not caused by vaccines has to do with the fact that children can be exposed to viruses even before birth. Scientists recently discovered that mothers can pass cells that cause diseases to their unborn children in the womb, and they suspect that the cells linger in the baby's system and can cause diseases later in life.

Scientists agree that until they know the cause (or causes) of autism, they cannot really cure it. They have looked at the disorder from many angles since it was first identified, and their studies have brought them closer than ever before to discovering its cause (or causes). They are optimistic that they will eventually find a cure and a way to prevent the disorder. In the meantime, they have experimented with different methods of treating symptoms, and those treatments have improved the quality of life for many autistics.

# Cognitive Functioning

Researchers have met with the greatest success in developing treatments by studying the way autistics understand the information that they receive from their senses (an area of study referred to as cognitive functioning). Psychologists use the term "cognition" to describe the way that people think about things, and they know that normal cognitive functioning allows people to understand the world around them well enough to behave normally. It allows them to pay attention to what is happening; to remember things from the past; to be aware of how things taste, look, feel, smell, and sound; to solve problems and make decisions; to think about experiences and to speak about them; and to imagine things and ideas that may not exist.

For reasons that are not completely understood, autistic individuals are not able to think in ways that are necessary to communicate normally, to share their experiences, and to express their feelings. They do not realize that other people have feelings, beliefs, and needs of their own because they cannot imagine anything that they do not personally experience. That may be why they cannot understand someone else's behavior and have a difficult time making friends.

Studies have shown that many autistics are better at understanding what they touch, taste, smell, and see than what they hear. This may be why parents often believe at first that their autistic child is deaf. It may also explain why many autistic children learn to speak later than other children and why they have trouble speaking normally.

Scientists are still not sure whether autism causes the differences in the autistic's cognitive thinking or the differences in cognitive thinking cause autism. Regardless of which causes which, they have discovered that autistics can be trained to react to their senses more normally, which helps them to function better in society. Such training programs help autistic children become more sensitive to what they hear and help them better organize the information that they receive through all of their senses. Although these programs won't cure the disorder, autistic children can benefit from them, and their behavior often improves over time.

*Oblivious to his surroundings, an autistic child stares intently at a light. Autistics have difficulty processing incoming stimuli and may focus on one object in order to prevent sensory overload.*

In an unusual but well-known case, one autistic woman designed her own method of treatment for sensory overload. When Temple Grandin was eighteen years old, she created what is now known as a "squeeze machine" to help her calm down when she felt overwhelmed and agitated by noise or other sensory input. She remembers:

> While visiting my aunt's ranch, I observed that cattle being handled in a squeeze chute sometimes relaxed after the pressure was applied. A few days later I tried the cattle squeeze

chute, and it provided relief for several hours. The squeeze machine was modeled after a squeeze chute used on cattle. It had two functions: (1) to help relax my "nerves" and (2) to provide the comforting feeling of being held.[19]

The squeeze machine is lined with foam rubber, and the user has complete control over the duration and amount of pressure applied. Squeeze machines are now used successfully in clinics to soothe autistic and hyperactive children.

## Medications

While cognitive therapies help some autistics, others benefit from taking prescription medications. Scientists studying the brain have discovered that some people with autism do not have enough serotonin, which is a chemical that plays an important role in normal brain functioning. Doctors have found that when autistic patients take medications that affect the level of serotonin in the brain, certain behaviors may improve.

Tranquilizers, which are drugs used to calm people down, are useful in treating autistics who are very aggressive, who tend to fight and throw tantrums. Many autistics have trouble falling asleep or sleeping throughout the night, and they are given medications called sedatives to help them sleep. Anticonvulsant medications help autistics who have seizures, which are brief episodes of blackouts accompanied by involuntary movements of the legs and arms.

Another treatment that seems to be effective is a substance called secretin, which is a chemical produced in the intestine to aid in digestion. In 1996 the mother of an autistic boy named Parker reported that shortly after taking a drug containing secretin, her son showed remarkable signs of recovery. In an interview with the BBC news, she said, "He was a totally non-responsive child who [was soon] able to concentrate on specific tasks. . . . He was able to sleep nights and became potty trained."[20]

Since then, parents of many other autistic children who have taken secretin have reported excellent results. Scientists, however, have just begun to test the effects of secretin on autistic children and believe that more research must be done before they will know exactly how much secretin will help and whether it is entirely safe. One researcher concluded that although some doctors who have experimented with the drug are enthusiastic about the results, it has not worked for all of the children it has been tried on. He adds, "It's not a miracle cure, but it makes sense and we are hopeful."[21]

None of these medications help all people with autism, and some people with autism don't take any medications at all. They are usually just one part of the autistic's treatment plan.

## Vitamins

Another part of the autistic's treatment plan might involve adding vitamin supplements to the diet. Scientists do not know exactly how vitamins work, but they know that they protect people's health and ensure that children grow properly. Without vitamins, many important chemical reactions in the body would slow down or stop. A well-balanced diet contains all the vitamins a healthy person needs, but people who are suffering from certain disorders often need to take additional vitamins, usually in the form of pills.

Many studies have shown that taking extra vitamins can help some people with autism. According to autism expert Dr. Bernard Rimland, at least eighteen different studies have tested the effects of adding vitamins to the diet of autistic children, and all "showed a remarkably wide range of benefits from the vitamin $B_6$. There was better eye contact, . . . more interest in the world around them, fewer tantrums, more speech, and in general the children became more normal, although they were not completely cured."[22] Still, despite vitamin $B_6$'s dramatic effects on some autistics, it does not help everyone who has autism.

## Changes in Diet

Many doctors recommend other changes in diet to treat some of the symptoms of autism. In general, people with autism have more allergies than the average person, and they are especially

*Possible Causes and Treatments*

*Studies have shown that many people with autism can benefit from taking vitamin supplements, especially vitamin $B_6$.*

sensitive to certain types of foods. The most common foods they are allergic to are grains, especially wheat, rye, and oats; dairy products; and foods that are often consumed during the spring and summer, particularly strawberries and citrus fruit. In autistics, these food sensitivities seem to be responsible for physical and behavioral problems like headaches, stomachaches, stuttering, excessive whining and crying, sleeping problems, temper tantrums, and intestinal problems (gas, diarrhea, constipation). These foods can also cause changes in the allergic person's physical appearance, including pink or black circles or bags under the

*Many autistics are especially sensitive to dairy products and other types of food, and often show improved behavior when these foods are eliminated from their diet.*

eyes, rosy cheeks or ears, rapid heartbeat, shallow breathing, and excessive perspiration.

The easiest way to find out if a particular food is causing a certain reaction is to eliminate the food from one's diet for a week or two. If the person is sensitive to the food, then there will be an improvement in the way the person feels and behaves when the food is no longer in the system. Once the food allergy is identified, the best way to treat it is to remove the food from the person's diet completely.

Researchers have conducted studies that show that many autistic children sensitive to wheat and milk products show a reduction in physical discomfort and improved behavior when they do not eat those foods. In addition, a food substance called DMG (dimethylglycine) seems to be an effective treatment for some people with autism. DMG has been tested on laboratory animals, and scientists discovered that the animals given DMG did a much better job of fighting off infection than those who did not receive it. The results of these studies also suggest that weaknesses in the immune system may be a cause of autism.

## Genetics

While some scientists focus their efforts on causes and cures, others look to the possibility of one day preventing the disorder. Scientists now know enough about genetics to be close to identifying which genes cause which traits, and they think that one day they will be able to look at people's DNA and tell them which health problems they are likely to have and to pass on to their children. When that happens, parents may be able to find out ahead of time whether their children are likely to be autistic. That would help them to make decisions about planning their family. And if a gene or genes can be identified as causing autism, then perhaps one day scientists will also be able to repair the broken gene and prevent the disorder from developing.

Current treatments include behavior modification, medication, vitamins, and special diets, and as one expert notes: "The fact that there are 20 treatments, none of which really work, is proof that we don't know what causes autism."[23] There is no cure, but today, more than ever before, people with autism can be helped. And many scientists are dedicated to understanding how the various regions of the brain work and developing preventive measures and new treatments for disorders like autism that handicap people in school, work, and social relationships.

# Chapter 3

# Options for Autistic Children

F OR MANY YEARS parents relied upon psychiatric hospitals to evaluate, diagnose, and treat their autistic children. Those parents who were able to care for and educate their autistic children at home would schedule regular appointments with doctors at the hospital to get help in understanding the needs of their child and learning what they could do to provide proper training. If the child's behavior worsened, the parents might have the child stay in the hospital for a week or two to be evaluated. Sometimes the parents would have the child remain in the hospital simply to allow the rest of the family to enjoy a brief respite, perhaps to take a short vacation without having to attend to the autistic child's special needs.

Families who were not able to provide much care and education for their autistic children at home sent them to live in mental hospitals or institutions, designed to help disabled children, or they enrolled them in private day schools for the disabled. Often these facilities were not equipped to offer high-quality education, however, because no clear standards had been set and the teachers had not been trained in special techniques to help disabled children learn.

In the 1970s the U.S. government passed a law that said disabled children in the public schools, including autistics, have a right to the same education that nondisabled students receive in order to reach their full potential. In response, educators developed appropriate curriculum and methods to meet the unique needs of autistic children. These educational programs have been adopted by all public schools and most private schools, so autistic children now have many more options than they did in the past for learning basic daily skills, getting an academic education, improving their physical coordination and social skills, and planning for the kind of life they will have as adults.

The key to helping the autistic child succeed is early diagnosis; the sooner parents and doctors recognize that a child has autism, the sooner parents and teachers can begin to give the child necessary special assistance. The earlier that children receive the right kind of educational assistance, the better they will do later in life. According to Geoffrey Cowley, reporting in *Newsweek*, "Only 10 percent of the autistic children entering the

*A 1970s law guaranteeing disabled children the same education as nondisabled students paved the way for special educational programs for autistic children, like this one in New York City.*

celebrated Princeton Child Development Center after age 5 go on to enter mainstream schools—yet half of those recognized earlier end up making the transition."[24] Parents whose autistic children have been diagnosed before the age of five often enroll their children in preschool programs that specialize in helping disabled children, including those with autism. In some cases, parents enroll in programs designed to teach them how to instruct their autistic children at home.

## The EarlyBird Programme

One such program is England's EarlyBird Programme, developed by the National Autistic Society to provide training for the parents of autistic children who are too young to start school. The National Autistic Society hopes to "lessen the frustration which can result from a child being misunderstood and remove the desperation and helplessness which parents sometimes feel."[25] Over a period of three months, instructors teach parents to "recognize and anticipate their child's behavior." They begin by documenting on videotape the child's reaction to a number of toys. One participant reported that "using techniques like looking at the video tape, the EarlyBird programme allowed us to get inside Tom's head and to understand the way he thought."[26]

The instructors know that it is easier for autistic children to understand what is being said to them if it is said in the order that things are going to happen, so they teach the parents to communicate accordingly. One mother explained that as a result of the training, "I would never dream of saying to him now, 'Tom, we're going to the park so you'd better get your coat on and get in the car.' I say to him, 'Tom, coat, car, park' and he understands the sequence of events."[27]

The instructors also teach the parents and children to use Picture Exchange Communication System (PECS) cards, which show pictures of objects like French fries, shoes, or pencil and paper and actions like a hug or a smile. When the children present a card, they receive the item or the action depicted on it. In this way they learn that they can communicate without words and that communication has its rewards.

Parents who participate in the program say that another benefit is the support they get from one another. Tom's mother remarked, "It's really nice to be able to talk to the other mothers. They all know what it's like and we have a lot of shared experiences."[28]

In the United States there are many programs like the Early-Bird Programme in which autistic infants, toddlers, and young children up to ages five or six go to class with their parents for a few hours a day. Other programs provide day care services just for young disabled and autistic children. These programs are offered by local school districts and by private facilities in the community. Children go to school for four hours each day, either in the morning or the afternoon, and they spend time with three or four teachers and six or seven other children.

One of these programs is the Children's Toddler School run by Children's Hospital and Health Center in San Diego, California. The school uses the "inclusion" approach to teaching disabled

*A teacher reads to a six-year-old autistic student. The earlier that an autistic child is diagnosed and receives educational assistance, the better he or she will do in school and later life.*

children, which means that children who are not disabled play and learn alongside children who are autistic. In order to be put in an inclusive class, the autistic child must have at least some ability to play independently without a teacher's constant attention. Children who can keep themselves busy, for example, by picking up blocks or rolling a toy car around on their own are usually able to be in a class with nondisabled children.

However, the goal of the class is not simply play for its own sake. The children are required to use language and to play with others in order to improve communication and social skills. The nondisabled children benefit from this experience because they enjoy helping their autistic friends, who don't speak or do other things for themselves. In addition, the nondisabled children often have more advanced language skills than other children the same age when they leave the toddler program because the smaller class size means they get more attention from their teachers.

Besides classroom activities, preschool programs often provide classes for parents, teaching them more about autism and how to help their children. A teacher may visit the autistic child's home for an hour or two each week to show the parents how to teach the child some of the same things that are taught in the classroom. Often the programs offer classes for the brothers and sisters of autistic children, who usually have questions about how they should treat their autistic sibling and about their own feelings, which are often complicated and confusing.

## Being in School

After completing their preschool education, autistic children enter kindergarten. Depending on the preferences of their parents, they may attend public or private school. They enroll in a special education classroom, a "mainstream" or normal classroom, or a combination of both. Each autistic student is different, and the parents work with professionals to determine what approach will work best for their individual child.

In order to be in a mainstream classroom, autistic children must be able to speak fairly well and have average or higher

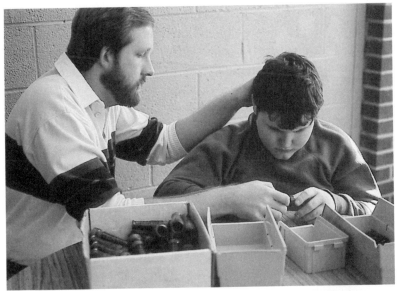

*A special education therapist works with an autistic boy. Autistic students benefit from educational programs designed specifically to meet their individual needs.*

intelligence. Those with serious speaking problems and lower intelligence benefit more from being in a specialized class, also known as special education. Some autistic children spend part of the day in a mainstream classroom to learn the basic academic subjects like reading, writing, arithmetic, and social studies, and then spend part of the day in a special education class, where they work on their speaking, social, and daily living skills.

Special education classes are small, with about ten students working with one or more teachers. This allows teachers to spend more time with each student. Because each autistic child has a set of skills and behavior quite different from another autistic child, teachers design each student's program to fit his or her individual needs. There are different classes for each level of disability. However, each program includes some common approaches, goals, and activities. Teachers use what is called a behavioral approach to teaching, which means that they rely heavily on giving students a reward each time they do things correctly. The reward must be something that the child values, and it is given to the child immediately, or as soon as possible, following the child's correct response.

## The Stein Center

This rewards system is used at the Sam and Rose Stein Education Center in San Diego, California. There, when ten-year-old Tony was learning to say hello and good-bye to people correctly, his teacher told him to say good-bye to Nancy, who was sitting next to him, before he left the table. The teacher reminded Tony to say good-bye, to say Nancy's name ("Good-bye, Nancy"), and to look at Nancy as he did so. It took many tries before Tony mastered the skills, but when he did he was immediately rewarded with Gummi Bears, his favorite treat. His teacher explained that it would take quite awhile before Tony would be able to remember to do this on his own whenever he exits a conversation or a group.

The Stein Center has also found that videotaping autistic children doing something right is an effective way to reinforce desirable behavior. The children love to see themselves on video, and watching themselves complete an action correctly helps them to remember how and when to do it. Special education teachers use a lot of visual information to accompany lessons, and they also try to stick to the same schedule every day because they know that autistic children, who are easily upset by changes in routine, learn better that way.

In a therapy group that addresses social skills, the teacher might set a goal for one child to be able to sit next to someone for thirty seconds. Or the teacher may have two children play a board game that is too difficult for them, knowing that they will become frustrated, which gives them an opportunity to learn how to deal with their frustration in appropriate ways.

In addition to communication and social skills, autistic children learn basic functioning skills like tying their shoes, combing their hair, and washing their hands. The students also learn and practice daily living skills like washing dishes, sweeping floors, crossing the street, making a simple purchase, using the library, asking for help when necessary, identifying community signs, developing awareness of their own strength, and respecting community safety rules. Some of these are critical skills and may be difficult even for autistic children with average intelligence.

The students practice what they have learned by going on outings, perhaps to the grocery store to purchase food for lunch or to a public show in the park, or even to a movie matinee. Most autistic children won't sit in a movie theater for more than thirty minutes, though; they have very short attention spans.

Almost all autistic children, at the Stein Center and elsewhere, also receive speech therapy and occupational therapy. Speech therapy sessions allow autistic children to spend extra time reviewing and learning new ways to use speech to communicate, often practicing skills using the PECS cards. Occupational therapy allows autistic children to spend extra time learning how to sort out the information they receive from their senses. For example, a child at the Stein Center might be asked to stand on a balancing platform while trying to catch a ball. This requires being aware of more than one sense at a time, which is quite difficult for most autistic children.

## Other Services

Some private schools offer day classes to autistic children who have some special interests that can be developed to reach future occupational goals. One of the schools run by Autism Initiatives offers a hairdressing and beauty salon that its students can work in. Another teaches pottery, arts and crafts, computer skills, woodworking skills for making and restoring furniture, and silkscreen printing for making T-shirts and posters.

Most schools also provide training and support groups for parents and for siblings throughout the autistic child's school career. Having a child or sibling who is autistic is stressful for the entire family, and it is helpful to be able to talk with school staff about how the child is progressing as well as to explore whatever feelings the family members are experiencing. The brothers and sisters of autistic children may want to discuss their feelings with an adult who is not their parent. They may

*A mother writes words as her autistic son, who cannot write himself, attempts to spell them for her. Training and support groups are available to help parents cope with the challenges of raising an autistic child.*

sometimes feel embarrassed, discouraged, or angry. They may love their autistic brother or sister very much but may not always like having him or her around. They can talk safely about these feelings with one of the school's teachers and other members of the school-run sibling group. Parents and siblings who feel confident and comfortable with their situation are able to be more supportive of the autistic child.

## Schools for Severe Behavior Problems

Some autistic children have communication or behavior problems that are so severe that they cannot participate in a mainstream or special education classroom. These are children who cannot speak or who get so angry when they do not get their way that they lash out at others. They may yell insults at people or even assault them. These children require extra attention in order to learn how to communicate effectively and to manage their emotions in appropriate ways.

Public and private schools who find these students' behavior too disruptive refer them to private schools in the community whose goal is to teach the students to control their behavior sufficiently to return to their special education or mainstream classroom. In these schools there is one teacher for every student, so each student receives a great deal of attention. The students learn that it is not acceptable to yell at or hit people when they are upset; instead, they learn that they can go for a brief walk to cool down, talk with a friend or counselor about whatever is bothering them, or just close their eyes and take some deep breaths.

Most of the students in this type of school cannot speak or lack basic functional skills, but some are high functioning, speak well, and can play chess or do other things that require some special abilities. What they have in common is their inability to communicate and behave in appropriate ways. Although the primary emphasis at these schools is behavior change, both low- and high-functioning students also attend classes in areas like cooking, arts and crafts, swimming, and reading and writing. The success rate of these schools is very high. After spending two to five years in one of these schools, most of the students are ready to return to their former classrooms to continue their education.

## Special Friends Program

Although most autistic children now attend public schools, they still have little contact with nondisabled students. Because they are lacking in social skills and act differently, their fellow students may exclude them or tease them.

The Special Friends Program is designed to bridge the gap between nondisabled and autistic students. Its goal is to educate nondisabled children about autism and thereby improve their attitudes while improving the social skills of autistic children. "The programs encourage selected non-disabled students to become friendly with autistic students, and provide settings (pizza parties, video games, etc.) which the students can enjoy together,"[29] explains one expert. Prior to attending these events, the nondisabled students watch videos about the importance of friends to the disabled, and they participate in discussion groups and role-playing activities that help them to understand what it feels like to be disabled.

Sometimes students in the program attend physical education or art classes with the autistic students. In the physical education classes, the students play team sports like hopscotch, tug-of-war, Frisbee, jump rope, and Twister, which help the autistic children develop social skills and motor skills. In art class, students practice sign language and learn how autistic students use nonverbal communication systems such as PECS wallet cards. All of the children receive training in basic art concepts including shape, texture, and color; visit a children's museum together; and work as teams on art projects.

The Special Friends Program has yielded positive results. In the physical education classes, teachers found that autistic students displayed less inappropriate play behavior. And in the art classes, nondisabled students increased their interaction with the autistic students. Overall, the nondisabled students at schools with the Special Friends Program had much more positive attitudes toward autistic students than at schools without the program. Successful programs like this one have led some educators to promote a policy that would eliminate special education classes and require that all autistic children be enrolled in general education classrooms.

## Full Inclusion

Some experts believe that all autistic children should attend regular schools and be placed in mainstream classrooms, regardless of behavior problems or their level of functioning. They

> argue that it is ethically wrong to segregate autistic children; that they will benefit socially and academically from involvement with non-disabled students in a natural setting; and that the non-disabled students, in turn, will benefit from exposure to students with disabilities.[30]

Those who advocate full inclusion express concern that disabled students' human rights are being violated when labels like "handicapped," "retarded," or "autistic" are applied to them. These advocates feel that, once labeled, the students are discriminated

*Some people believe that autistic children benefit socially and academically by being placed in mainstream classrooms, like the one shown.*

against by being placed in special education classes that offer a different curriculum than mainstream classes. They compare this type of segregation to the historical social and educational segregation of African Americans in the United States.

In addition, many of these advocates report that when full-inclusion programs have enough funding to support small class size, adequate staffing levels, and special training for teachers and classroom aides, both disabled and nondisabled students benefit from the experience. Their hope is that nondisabled students who are in classrooms with children who have disabilities like autism will be more likely to express compassion for and accept people who are different from them. They also hope that nondisabled students who demonstrate appropriate behavior and social skills will be good role models for students who are autistic. Other benefits include those reported by education expert Diane Ranking:

> The inclusive classrooms I walked into had general education teachers who had the benefit of collaborative planning sessions and day to day team-teaching with special education teachers and specialists. I saw general and special education students learning and benefiting from what has been called the gift of inclusion. . . . I saw students in general education actively involved in solving real problems of including the student with severe disabilities and that student being functionally involved in his actual community of ten-year-old peers. I saw students in general education becoming intensely interested in how their peers with disabilities learned. I saw those same students beginning to be intensely interested in their own learning. I saw students who had difficulty learning a particular subject being inspired by the student with severe disabilities working hard to meet his own individual goal.[31]

Opponents of full inclusion agree that high-functioning autistic children may benefit from being in mainstream classrooms and argue that although "there is no scientific evidence proving that full inclusion is beneficial either to autistic or to non-disabled students,"[32] they should have the opportunity to be included. However, they make it clear that they object to making inclusion a mandatory policy, which is what many school boards across the country have tried to do. Instead, they urge educators to keep in mind the best interests of each autistic child. Special education consultant Laurence Lieberman warns that "full inclusion is not *the* right thing to do. It is one right thing to do, sometimes."[33]

Opponents like Lieberman argue that special education classes are vitally important to many low-functioning autistic children. There are known benefits of individualized instruction, intensive skills training, and other services offered to autistic children through special education, and those may outweigh the benefits of integration. Specialized training offers autistic children the opportunity to learn functional skills that are necessary for independent

*Most educators believe that autistic students do best with individualized instruction and skills training possible only in special education classes.*

adult life. Authors Richard Simpson and Gary Sasso point out that "young men and women with autism who leave school without job, self-care, and independent-living skills spend their lives in segregated settings more often than individuals who have acquired functional skills."[34] Therefore, they recommend that students be placed in full-inclusion settings only on a case-by-case basis, taking into consideration the teacher's willingness to tailor programs to the individual needs of students.

Simpson and Sasso add, however, that schools must also consider the needs of general education teachers and nondisabled students, arguing that "it is unrealistic to expect non-disabled students and regular education teachers and staff to independently and exclusively make all necessary adjustments to accommodate students with autism in full-time general education settings."[35] This concern has been echoed by representatives of America's two major teachers' organizations, the National Education Association (NEA) and the American Federation of Teachers (AFT). Members of both organizations are "disturbed by an escalating number of injuries to teachers caused by aggressive children with autism or other disabilities" enrolled in regular classrooms and feel that mandatory inclusion "endangers teachers by placing violent special education students on regular campuses with inadequate provisions for dealing with their behavior problems."[36]

In addition to voicing concerns about the physical dangers, educators question whether all disabled students can benefit from mainstreaming. The National Longitudinal Transition Study of Special Education Students reported that the disabled high school students who benefited most from full inclusion were those who were physically, hearing, or vision impaired. High school students with severe impairments such as autism, however, found no advantages in full inclusion. The study concluded: "This difference in impacts supports the hypothesis that regular education benefits youth cognitively equipped to absorb regular high school coursework."[37] Thus, until more is known about the possible benefits, many educators and parents of children with autism advocate that full-inclusion programs be considered experimental and as one of a variety of placement options.

Regardless of where and how they receive their education, many autistic children work hard in school and look forward to the time as an adult when they will be able to live as normal a life as possible. By the time they are eighteen years old, they are ready to prepare to get a job and decide where they will live.

# Chapter 4

# Options for Autistic Adults

A UTISTIC STUDENTS AND their families find that preparing to graduate and leave the education system is a critical planning task. They typically begin the process even earlier than most students because the factors they must consider are complex and concern the safety and survival of young people who are more physically and mentally vulnerable than most. Students receiving special education services in public schools hold frequent meetings with family and school staff to identify the student's abilities, needs, and goals. When students reach

---

*A mother and her nineteen-year-old autistic son, Dustin, talk with a reporter about Dustin's upcoming graduation from high school. For those with autism, a successful transition from high school to adult life requires a great deal of planning and preparation.*

high school, one purpose of these meetings is to plan for the transition from high school to adult life. Students, along with their families, teachers, and school counselors, decide whether they will pursue vocational education or a college education; whether they will seek employment or work as a volunteer in the community; and whether they will continue to live with their parents, move into a supervised living situation, or live independently.

## Transitional Programs

In order to make sure that each autistic student will be as well prepared for adulthood as possible, a federal law requires that written transition plans for disabled students be included in a document called an Individualized Education Program (IEP), which must be completed by the time the student is sixteen years old. An autistic student's IEP states specific plans, including the action steps and deadlines, for the student's move from school to future activities, including adult education, vocational (job-related) training, employment, independent living, and community participation. The activities in the student's plan are based on his or her needs, taking into account the student's abilities, preferences, and interests.

This planning process usually starts during junior high school, when autistic students and their families explore some career options. They visit with a school counselor to discuss interests and abilities. From there, the family can decide whether they want to plan for attending a regular college or a vocational school or neither. They'll read books, go to career fairs, and talk to people in the community to find out more about careers that seem interesting.

When thinking about the future, families and school staff try to understand as completely as possible what the autistic individual likes to do, and is able to do, as well as what he or she still needs to explore and learn to reach his or her goals. Because of the autistic's physical and mental impairments, the choices are far more limited than those of a nondisabled student. Families and professionals must consider whether the individual would be able to attend a community college or a four-year college, or

*Anna, who is autistic, plays on her high school softball team. Some high-functioning autistic students like Anna are able to go on to college and a career.*

would do better in vocational education or adult classes learning specific job-related skills. They have to determine whether the individual will be able to get a job and, if so, where he or she might go to find employment and training services. They also must consider practical concerns such as what type of transportation the individual is able to use, where the person will live, and how expenses will be paid. Health insurance may cover some expenses, and there are programs available to help with additional costs through the local Vocational Rehabilitation agency and the Social Security Administration if the student qualifies for disability assistance.

Because people with autism find it especially difficult to communicate effectively with people, it is equally important to consider whether the individual has friends and what kind of support might be needed to encourage forming additional friendships. Do people in the community know this person? What about making time for recreation, exercise, and even hobbies? Will there be opportunities to attend religious services and social events? Could the individual get involved in volunteer work? Most autistics need extra help from friends and other people in the community who know them and understand their limitations in order to lead a life that includes meaningful leisure and social activities as well as work.

In high school the autistic student, like any student, takes classes that are related to his or her future plans. These may be classes that are required to get into college or trade school or that help prepare one for a future career. Students might get involved in early work experiences by working part-time or in the summer or by doing volunteer work. The autistic student, however, is more likely to focus on learning one employment-related skill to the exclusion of many other academic subjects. For example, a student with autism who has particularly sharp computer skills might be dismissed from school early a few days a week to work with an aide at a data processing office. Before beginning the job, the student would be taught appropriate office social skills and important office procedures such as using a time clock. Another student who prefers to be outdoors might work with a community clean-up project. These experiences help to determine whether the student's plans are in fact a good fit for the individual's interests and abilities. The most important thing is that the IEP be used to actually prepare autistic students for their lives after high school.

Students who want to go to college or vocational school will identify which schools they want to attend and write for catalogs, financial aid information, and an application. Many private schools do not offer accommodations for people with learning disabilities, so the autistic's choices are limited. When they find a school they would like to attend, they will probably visit the school and contact the Office for Special Student Services or the Disabled Student Service Office. They will want to know whether there is a learning disability (LD) specialist on staff and how many LD students attend the college. They are unlikely to be able to live in a dormitory or sorority or fraternity house because they require additional supervision. An alternate method of transportation may be necessary if the student cannot drive or take the bus or subway to school. If so, they will need to find out if the school can make those accommodations. Autistic students will also need to take any tests for learning disabled individuals that are required for entry into the institution.

## Vocational Training and College

Higher-functioning autistics who want to attend college before going to work may spend a year or two developing work-related

*The rigorous demands of college coursework make it crucial that autistics who plan to attend college first develop good study skills and learn how to effectively manage their time.*

skills and interests before applying for college. This may involve taking some vocational courses at a local trade school or community college, where they will learn study skills in addition to learning more about how to do the kind of work that interests them. It is critical that autistic students know how to manage their time so that they can meet the requirements of all of their classes; how to listen to lectures and read textbooks so that they understand the information and can summarize it; how to participate in a class discussion; how to write an essay and a research paper; and how to take exams. These are skills that most college-bound students have mastered by the time they graduate from high school, usually at a higher level of proficiency than autistic students.

Autistic students headed for higher education also need to increase their independent living skills. They need to be able to do laundry, cleaning, and some cooking; manage a checking account; drive or take public transportation; and plan leisure activities. It requires much more practice for autistic students to learn these skills than it does for other students. Part-time jobs and volunteer positions offer additional opportunities to practice social skills and learn more about work situations and job expectations.

During this time, they will find out whether the college they hope to attend has a program for students with disabilities to accommodate their needs. By law, public schools must make it possible for disabled students to have the same access to their educational programs as nondisabled students. They often offer extra classes designed to help students with learning disabilities to read and study better. School counselors often recommend that autistic students enroll in a summer orientation session for learning disabled students or that they take one course in a regular summer session. "Getting acclimated to the campus and knowing about support service systems builds the student's confidence,"[38] a counselor explains. While a nondisabled student will also probably do better in college if he or she has done this kind of advance preparation, it is often critical to the autistic student's academic survival.

Only about one out of ten freshmen attending college in 1991 was disabled, and only about a quarter of those had learning disabilities, so it is clear that very few people with autism attend college. Those who do, however, seem to enjoy being there. However, the transition after college can be difficult. One educator observes that she knows of

> many sad cases of people with autism who have successfully completed high school or college but have been unable to make the transition into the world of work. Some have become perpetual students because they thrive on the intellectual stimulation of college. For many able people with autism college years were their happiest.[39]

She recommends that autistic college students make a gradual transition from the world of college to the world of work. It is a good idea to work for short periods while still in school and essential to find employers who are willing to work with people with autism.

## Adult Education

Since few autistic students go on to college or vocational school, most attend adult education programs in the community for low-functioning autistics between the ages of eighteen and twenty-two, some of whom also have behavioral problems. These programs provide additional time for planning and decision making as well as preparation for greater independence in the workplace. For example, the mission of the Supported Employment Services of San Diego is to assist students in becoming as skilled and as independent as possible through training in the community. The program teaches work and communication skills as well as behavior management and recreation and leisure skills.

This program builds on the autistic's strengths to find the right on-the job training placement. For example, someone who enjoys being outside and has a lot of stamina but has few skills in other areas may be placed in a job picking up litter. Students are paid for the on-the-job training they receive, so they learn budgeting skills as well as the concept of being rewarded for work.

*An autistic man works at a warehouse boxing batteries. People with autism are often well-suited for such repetitive, precise work.*

The students go to work in small groups, accompanied by one staff person for each student. One such group works for Sea World in San Diego, wiping trays and tables in one of its restaurants. Another group works in a park, wiping benches, cleaning trash can lids, and picking up litter. Yet another works at a pet supply store, cleaning the offices and rest rooms. And another group does sweeping, mopping, vacuuming, and weeding for the Naval Air Base on San Diego's North Island. One of the things the students like best about these jobs is that they get to wear the company's uniform, which makes them feel like they're just like the other employees.

Some of the students may not understand the value of money yet, but it means a lot to them to be able to interact with the public. Some learn about the value of money when they don't have enough to pay for something they want, and they may ask to work more hours for the extra pay. Others have no problem seeing the connection between going to work and having money and being able to buy the things they like. One young man who vacuums the interiors of cars for a local car wash had his eye on a compact disc player, and a teacher says she noticed that "the bigger his paycheck, the bigger the smile on his face"[40] as he saved up enough money to purchase it.

*Two autistic men make extra money by assembling pieces for car door locks. Working for a paycheck helps teach autistics about the value of money and gives them a sense of self-satisfaction.*

# Employment Opportunities

Autistic adults who have experienced success in a transitional program like the Supported Employment Services of San Diego or who have completed vocational training or college usually go on to enter one of two types of employment programs. Lower-functioning autistics usually become part of a sheltered work program, which provides very basic vocational training along with training in other skill areas such as self-help and recreation. In a typical program, autistic adults between the ages of twenty-two and fifty-nine are employed from ten to fifteen hours a week, working in groups of three and supervised 100 percent of the time by a job coach.

The role of the job coach is to make sure that autistic employees arrive at work on time and leave on time; that they dress appropriately; that they wear name tags, hats, or uniforms if they are supposed to; that they perform satisfactory work; and that they interact appropriately with their supervisors and coworkers. Autistic employees like to feel that they fit in with their nondisabled coworkers, so the job coach shows them how to do that by, for example, making sure they eat lunch with their coworkers in the lunchroom.

When not at work, their job coach works with them on other skills. They learn to take public transportation between home and the program center, and some can get to and from the program by themselves. They practice saying "hello" and "goodbye" to people and behaving appropriately in public. They learn to purchase a meal in a cafeteria, and their job coach takes them to the neighborhood where they live to practice making purchases at the grocery store so that they can buy a few things independently. This requires that they build relationships with some of the people in their neighborhood. Often the job coach introduces them to the store manager and one or two cashiers, who will keep a watchful eye out for them.

Many well-known employers in the community make special arrangements to employ the participants in these programs. For example, students at the Stein Center Assisted Employment Services Program have jobs in companies like Sears, Wal-Mart,

*With the assistance of a job coach, this autistic man works making boxes at a warehouse. Job coaches help their autistic clients remain responsible and productive workers.*

Tower Records, Hollywood Videos, and Mann Theatres. One group of employees sorts checks at a local fast-food chain. One employee, who is confined to a wheelchair, fills salt and pepper shakers, grates cheese, and assembles boxes for a Domino's Pizza restaurant. Those program participants who lack other skills can help with mailings for employers—sorting, stapling, folding, stuffing envelopes, and applying mailing labels and stamps. Everyone gets paid, and the workers take pride in their accomplishments.

Autistics who function at a higher level than those participating in the sheltered work programs are eligible to participate in supported employment programs, which are designed to serve individuals who have the desire and potential to be employed independently in the workplace. The program finds a job for and trains each employee. The individuals entering this type of program usually have prepared for it by attending a trade or vocational school. Initially the job coaches work closely with the employees and their supervisors at work, but gradually they reduce the amount of time they spend with employees until they finally come by the workplace to check on them only about six to eight hours each month. These employees do best at jobs that are highly structured and repetitious, so they might work as piano tuners, painters, farmworkers, office workers, computer operators, dishwashers, or assembly line workers.

## Living Arrangements

Once some decisions have been made about obtaining additional education or vocational skills and entering the workforce, autistic students are equally concerned about where they will live as adults. People with autism typically live at home until they are at least twenty-one years old and have completed their education and transitional programs. At that point, many families begin to consider other living options. In the past, parents' choices were limited to keeping their autistic children at home or placing them in large institutions with other disabled people. Today parents can choose from four main types of residential settings depending on the autistic's needs and abilities to live independently.

Institutions are still an option for some people with autism. Although many people think of institutions as places that are large and unfriendly, where residents are treated with a lack of care and understanding, generalizations like this are often untrue. The quality of care at both private and public institutions varies, and families usually investigate their choices thoroughly before making a decision to place their children there.

An institution is an appropriate place for an adult with autism if it meets needs that no other setting can provide. It may offer safety and protection for autistic adults who tend to injure themselves or who like to run away or wander off. It may also offer rigid schedules and fixed routines for those who respond well to a high degree of predictability and security. On the other hand, there is usually less privacy and less interaction with nondisabled adults than in other places that autistic people can live.

Adult foster care is an option that may appeal to many families and individuals with autism. The individual lives in a home with a family and other people with or without disabilities. Unlike foster care for younger children, adult foster care is meant to be as permanent as possible. The families who open their homes to adults with disabilities receive government money, but are not necessarily trained or expected to teach individuals independent living skills or behavior modification. Adult foster care homes may be best suited to adults who do not require extensive supervision and assistance.

A skill development home is similar in many ways to an adult foster care home. The adult individual with autism lives with a family in their home. The family receives compensation from the agency responsible for the individual's care. However, unlike a foster family, the family in a skill development home is trained to work with a person's specific disability. The family members are expected to teach self-care skills and housekeeping and assist with the development of recreation or leisure activities.

For autistic adults who require less training than those in skill development homes, supervised group living has become a popular choice. A group home is a facility that usually serves several individuals with disabilities. These homes are typically located in residential neighborhoods and appear no different from an average family home. The homes are staffed by trained professionals who assist residents based on each person's level of need. This can include teaching personal care skills, housekeeping, and meal preparation. Usually the residents have some type of job, which takes them away from home during the day. The group home may not be specific to autism; most include residents with different types of disabilities. Some group homes do specialize in serving adults with autism, and the staff in those homes are trained to address the unique needs associated with autism.

A supervised apartment may be the choice for individuals who prefer to live with fewer people but still require some supervision and assistance. In these situations, a staff person does not usually provide daily supervision, but comes one or two times a week. The residents are responsible for going to work, preparing meals, and personal care and housekeeping needs. A supervised apartment setting might be appropriate for an individual who is preparing to make the transition to independent living.

*Residents of a group home for autistic men exercise and fold laundry. Supervised group homes are staffed by trained professionals who are able to assist residents based on their individual needs.*

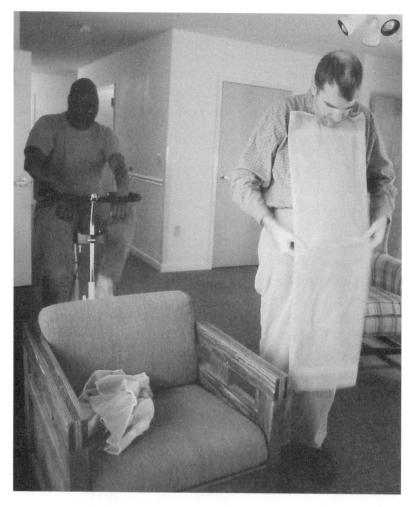

Independent living as a residential option means just that: individuals live in their own apartments or houses and require little, if any, support services from outside agencies. Services may be limited to helping individuals with complex problems rather than day-to-day living skills. For example, individuals may need assistance with money management or with handling local, state, or federal government bureaucracies. This option is best suited for those who have developed appropriate social and daily living skills and are capable of taking care of their own necessities.

All of these living options are available in large cities in the United States, and many of them can be found in smaller cities as well. Some adults with autism prefer to live in a rural setting, however, and there are satisfying living arrangements for them to do so.

## The Rural Alternative

One of the reasons that some autistics prefer the rural life is the high crime rate in many cities. As distressing as it would be for a nondisabled person to be robbed or assaulted, it is even worse for someone who is disabled. In addition, as one expert points out, "Being lost or even losing keys or missing a bus can be an immensely more traumatic event for the autistic person than for the rest of us."[41]

Another advantage of rural life is that the type of work available on a farm or ranch may be preferable to that available in the city. A person with autism may consider taking care of farm animals and growing vegetables to be more rewarding than working in a factory, restaurant, or office. The father of an autistic son says:

> This is certainly so in Mark's case. Mark has compiled and stapled innumerable papers, stuffed innumerable envelopes, licked and affixed countless stamps, and performed a great deal of other kinds of repetitive office work. He does it willingly, but he doesn't really like it, and considers it boring. . . . We want Mark's life and work to be as rewarding as possible.[42]

There are a number of farms and ranches for autistic adults and teenagers in the United States and in other countries. In one

*An autistic man from a group home receives help from a staff member while shopping for clothes. Most autistic adults need lifelong training, assistance, and supervision.*

such community, residents work a five-hour day doing greenhouse, farming and household chores; raising poultry; caring for livestock; and keeping up the buildings. One father of an autistic adult believes that part of the appeal of this kind of setting is that many disabled people prefer to be around others with similar disabilities, explaining:

> I am all too well aware of once happy handicapped individuals whose lives have been made miserable by their being "integrated" into a work situation, usually in a supported employment setting, where they feel isolated and excluded from the conversations and social activities of their non-handicapped coworkers. Imagine being dropped into a setting where people functioned at an intellectual level perhaps 50 or more IQ points above yours, where their comments, jokes and conversations occurred on a level far above your capacity to comprehend, and where your infrequent inclusion into their activities and conversations was largely a function of their kindness and patience. Not very satisfactory—at least from our family's point of view.[43]

Regardless of their choice of education, employment, and living arrangements, most adults with autism need lifelong training, ongoing supervision, and reinforcement of skills. Today about one-third of autistic adults can live and work in the community with some degree of independence. As communities and employers become more aware of the potential contributions of autistic individuals, their options continue to expand.

# Chapter 5

# The Autistic Savant and Asperger's Syndrome

Psychologists have found it especially fascinating to study two groups of autistic individuals in particular—the autistic savants and those suffering from Asperger's syndrome. The members of the first group exhibit some of the cognitive abilities of a genius despite the fact that their intelligence, language, and social skills may be severely impaired. The members of the second group exhibit normal intelligence and language development accompanied by autistic-like behaviors and marked deficiencies in social and communication skills. Members of both groups usually fail to fully realize their potential because they are unable to live and work effectively in mainstream society. By studying these individuals, however, scientists have developed a better understanding of the way all humans think and relate to one another socially.

## Autism and Genius

Researchers have come to recognize that the unusual interests and skills of those with autism are, in some cases, the mark of a genius. An expert tells of one such young man:

> Curtis is a genius in mathematics. He can multiply, add and subtract huge numbers in his head. He figures out instantly

which product is the best buy in the supermarket. He is also a calendar calculator. He can tell you what day of the week that a date many years away will fall. Early in his childhood he had an unusual ability for identifying kinds of cars. This was when he was only 18 months old, and along with it he had the ability to spell, read and memorize.[44]

Autistic children like Curtis have often been referred to as "idiot savants," a term meaning a retarded person who can perform various mental feats that a normal person cannot. The name is misleading, however; a scientist who studies autism points out that "rarely, if ever, though, is the IQ actually at the idiot level (below 30). The term is actually from the French *idiot*, which means ill informed or untutored rather than stupid. Because the children we are talking about are autistic rather than retarded, we prefer to call them autistic savants."[45]

Although a minority, there are savants who are both autistic and retarded; they continue to be referred to as idiot savants.

*This painting was done by autistic savant Mark Rimland, the son of autism expert Bernard Rimland. Autistic savants display remarkable abilities in areas such as art, mathematics, and language.*

Researchers have determined an autistic savant is more likely to have special skills in several areas than an idiot savant; more than half of all autistic savants have two or more savant abilities. For example, Peter

> has apparently total recall for statistics, such as baseball, football, hockey, basketball scores, individual records, etc. He knows capitals and heads of governments for all countries of the world, their flags, can make a good outline map of any of them (and keep them current). He reads almanacs, encyclopedias and dictionaries. You never have to look anything up if Peter is around. He remembers dates, birthdays, etc. He seems also to be quite artistic—draws quite well, and the last couple of years has shown some originality (not much but a step forward). Is inclined to copy. Peter could do calendar calculating, but won't do it anymore. He could draw an outline of the 48 states and place the capital cities when he was two years old. He writes beautifully in Japanese, can print old English as fast as he can print normally. He has a working knowledge of French, Spanish, Japanese and Russian—knows at least the alphabet and pronunciations of Arabic, Hebrew and several others.[46]

Savant abilities do not appear in all autistic children or only in autistic children, although amazing mental abilities do appear more often in autistic people than in members of any other group. Some severely retarded individuals and some nonretarded individuals (usually those who have suffered a brain injury or disease) have savant abilities, and there are those few who can be considered true geniuses.

Researchers note that

> a number of people at the genius or near-genius level in the "normal" population have also exhibited some signs of autism. Many of the eccentricities—the "absent-minded professor" habits—of geniuses such as Newton and Einstein fall into the category of autistic traits. . . . The brilliant inventor and entrepreneur Howard Hughes was reported to have kept a ruler

near at hand during his last two years to make sure that the chocolate cakes he had delivered to him each day measured exactly 12 inches on each side.[47]

Canadian pianist Glenn Gould "was notorious for his bizarre behavior: he had a phobia about shaking hands, ate nothing

*Canadian pianist Glenn Gould was notorious for his eccentric behavior. His strange obsessions and incessant rocking at the piano are common autistic traits.*

but scrambled eggs and arrowroot biscuits, and rocked incessantly at the keyboard."[48] When Bobby Fischer won the World Chess Championship, his eccentric behavior also attracted special attention and comment because he spent his time during the awards ceremony working out chess problems on his miniature board, quite oblivious to the activities going on around him.

## Savants in the Media

Recent books, television shows, and movies have increased public awareness of the subject of savants. In her book *Nadia: A Case of Extraordinary Drawing Ability in an Autistic Child*, Lorna Selfe explains that Nadia, at the age of six and a half, was taken by her mother to a specialist at the Child Development Research Unit at Nottingham University in England. Nadia could barely speak and was doing poorly at a local school for retarded children. Her mother mentioned during the interview that Nadia liked to draw and showed some of her drawings to the interviewer. In his review of the book, Dr. Bernard Rimland describes the university interviewer as being

> stunned by what she saw. Few of us would not have been stunned, for Nadia's untutored drawings provide us with a totally unexpected and tantalizing glimpse of extraordinary artistic genius. Any normal 6-year-old would have been hailed as a creative prodigy for producing these pictures. But Nadia? Nadia, a clumsy, lethargic, impassive child who hardly knew her own name? . . . Nadia had just started drawing at about 3-1/2 years of age. She reportedly didn't scribble, just began drawing recognizable objects from the "moment she put pen to paper."[49]

By the time Nadia was ten years old, which is about the time the book was published, her speaking abilities had improved, she could count, and she had learned some social skills. Strangely, however, her drawing ability faded as she acquired new skills. A television documentary on Nadia and some articles published soon thereafter took the position that the decline of her drawing skills was the result of the training Nadia had received in language, and that the development of left [brain] hemisphere skills . . . had robbed her of the precious, presumably right-hemispheric, drawing skills. We will never know the answer. . . .[50]

Other autistic savants who have been reported on in the media are Richard Wawro and Leslie Lemke, both of whom appeared on the television show *That's Incredible!* and were the subjects of two *Reader's Digest* articles. A gifted artist,

Richard is legally blind and has many other handicaps. He can speak only to a limited degree, and at age 30 was just beginning to write his name. Nevertheless, he has produced beautiful "paintings" (actually done with artist's crayons) that have been displayed in one-man shows throughout Europe and the United States. Richard, like Nadia, . . . showed his precocious artistic ability in early childhood.[51]

Unlike those of Richard Wawro, Leslie Lemke's unusual abilities were not apparent until adulthood. Lemke is described by Bernard Rimland and Deborah Fein in "Special Talents of Autistic Savants":

Leslie was born without eyes, and was severely crippled with cerebral palsy. The infant, totally unresponsive to light, sound, or touch, was abandoned by his parents. A nurse, May Lemke, adopted him and devoted her life thereafter to caring for this helpless individual. She was able to get Leslie to stand by himself for the first time at age 16. He had no speech and few desires. His first sentence was spoken in his mid-20s, and at age 28 he "began talking in earnest." As the story is told, May and her husband were awakened at 3 A.M. on a winter morning in 1971, when Leslie was about 20 years old, by the sound of Tchaikovsky's Piano Concerto No. 1 being played on the piano. It was Leslie, who had never played nor shown interest in the piano before. Leslie soon turned out to be a remarkably good musician, both on the piano and in singing.[52]

A fictionalized account of his life has also been televised.

*Doctor Bernard Rimland is an autism expert who has worked with and written extensively about autistic savants.*

Additional media attention was drawn to the subject of autism by Dustin Hoffman's Academy Award–winning portrayal of Raymond Babbit in *Rain Man* (1988). Hoffman's character is based upon the lives of autistic savants with whom autism expert Bernard Rimland works. Rimland notes that *Rain Man* "brought about a huge upsurge in awareness and understanding of autism."[53] Such awareness has generated widespread curiosity about the phenomenal abilities of the autistic savant.

## How Do They Do It?

Researchers continue to be baffled by how the autistic savant's mind differs from the average person's mind. One well-known scientist explains that normal people are able to focus on both details and broad concepts, choosing between the two as necessary to complete a task. He points out, however, that an individual cannot do both at the same time. He refers to the processing of fine details as "high-fidelity" thinking and offers the following example:

> If you were given ten minutes to study a book, you could choose to memorize verbatim the first paragraph or two (high fidelity information processing) or you could instead choose to skim the chapter titles and first few sentences of each chapter to get a conceptual overview of the book. The choice is yours: focus on high fidelity *physical* stimuli (letters or words), or instead focus on lower fidelity, but conceptually richer ideas and concepts.[54]

According to this scientist, the savant mind "is perpetually locked into the concrete, high fidelity mode, which permits (compels) him to deal with numbers, sounds, and other physical data with great precision . . . at the cost of the ability to deal with concepts."[55] Normal minds, he explains, have difficulty achieving and

*Dustin Hoffman's portrayal of an autistic savant in* Rain Man *(pictured), was credited with increasing public awareness and understanding of autism.*

remaining in the high-fidelity mode. When most people try to concentrate on solving a challenging math problem, they are likely to be distracted by thoughts about, for example, what they will have for lunch or whether they remembered to lock the door behind them when they left home for work that morning. The savant,

> locked into his (relatively) distraction-free world, is oblivious to what we call reality. His reality is of a different sort—one we can rarely and fleetingly enter. His skills are those achieved by the computer, tape recorder, and camera—devices which process data precisely and without distraction.[56]

Because of their unique abilities, autistic savants who also function better than the majority of autistics often are diagnosed with Asperger's syndrome and seek more specialized education and support than that which is provided for other autistic individuals.

## Asperger's Syndrome

Asperger's syndrome is a disorder at the less severe end of the autistic spectrum, and some people who have it may also possess savant abilities. Approximately 10 percent of autistic children and adults are diagnosed with Asperger's syndrome, which, like autism, affects four to five times as many boys as girls. People with Asperger's syndrome usually have average to high intelligence but are regarded as odd or eccentric. They speak in a stilted, robotic manner and have strong interests in a limited few topics (like maps, trains, or the weather), but show little interest in biography, history, psychology, and other people-oriented topics. They communicate poorly, standing too close and talking too loudly or too long. It is difficult for them to develop friendships and interact cordially with other people.

Hans Asperger, who first diagnosed the disorder in 1944, felt that it was separate from autism because people with Asperger's are usually more intelligent and less disturbed than those with autism, have unique abilities, first show symptoms after the age of three, and develop highly grammatical speech very early. Recent research, however, has convinced many professionals to focus on the core similarities between Asperger's and autism. Both types of individuals have "problems with social interaction, with communication and with play."[57] Therefore, most experts now prefer to use the term "Asperger's syndrome" to describe those with autism who have extremely good verbal skills and are far less withdrawn than other autistics.

Researchers have noticed that those with Asperger's syndrome express their social problems in a variety of ways. "For example," observes one expert, "instead of being socially aloof and indifferent, the classic autistic picture, some children made active social approaches to others, but in a naïve, hopelessly inappropriate way." Although the children may have perfect grammar and a large vocabulary, she continues, "they used this to talk on and on in a monotonous way about pet subjects." Their voices tend to be flat and emotionless. One mother describes her child's speech as "so unlike normal speech, not because of any particular defect, but because it seems to be without joy and to lack life."[58]

*Ten percent of the autistic population is diagnosed with Asperger's syndrome. People with this syndrome are usually male, have superior verbal skills, and are less withdrawn than other autistics.*

People with Asperger's syndrome are no better than other autistics at interpreting body language and facial expressions. In one study, it was difficult for them to identify emotions when they were shown pictures of people who were angry, frightened, or sad. According to one researcher who studied seven children with Asperger's syndrome, their inability to understand and follow the rules of social behavior meant they "were unable to form lasting friendships and children refused to return to their homes to play with them."[59] Over time, these children avoided social interaction and retreated into the safety of their families. They felt rejected but did not know how or why they had become outcasts.

Children with Asperger's tend to think almost constantly about certain subjects that they find interesting. This intense need to dwell on these subjects is called a fixation or an obsession. One child might know everything there is to know about tornados. Another child might memorize entire TV shows and recite them over and over. Some "specialize in memorizing everything there is to know about the oddest things: deep-fat fryers, telephone cable insulating companies, the passengers on the *Titanic*, exotic species of cicadas, the provincial capitals of Brazil. In one documented case, a child memorized the birthdays of every member of Congress."[60] It is not unusual to find that many individuals with Asperger's are capable of doing things that most people cannot.

## Training, Education, and Support Groups

As educators have come to recognize that many autistic children are not retarded and that, in fact, many have special skills and abilities, more effective training has become available to all autistics, especially those with Asperger's syndrome. One teacher points out that, for many, inclusion in regular classrooms doesn't work because the autistic children do not have the opportunity to work on improving communication and social skills. She says,

> We feel that we need to get to the Asperger's children as early
> as possible in order to get through to them. When we teach

them the facial expression charts here, they are all learning the same thing. When we make them focus and maintain eye contact, they all have to do it. It doesn't make them feel abnormal.[61]

One pioneer in the education of autism and Asperger's syndrome is Dr. Richard L. Simpson. He reports having had positive results using "social scripts" and "social autopsies." A social autopsy follows a social incident that went badly. The teacher will sit down with the student to review what happened and discuss what can be done in the future in a similar situation. As an example, he recalls a high school student who

> would carry around the disciplinary code at his school. Actually, he had the entire code memorized. During break time and between classes, he would approach groups of kids and start spouting out the rules of the school, verbatim. This was a problem because the other kids would blow him off or provoke him. I know that some of his teachers started using scripts which involved teaching him to say more appropriate things or knowing when not to speak. This was not completely successful. But then we worked with the peers and told them what to say when this student began talking about the school's disciplinary code, such as "not appropriate" or "not here," the student was quite responsive and was more accepted by his high school peers. [62]

Teachers also find it important to accurately assess the student's skills in all areas on a frequent basis. Because Asperger's children often relate well to adults and even sound like adults because of their vocabulary, mastery of grammar, and academic knowledge, their teachers often forget that some of their other skills may be weak. They may give the impression of being very bright because they have relied on rote learning and memory, but in reality their ability to comprehend and apply what they know may be quite poor. When these children fail to get help in all of the required areas, they begin to have difficulties in school. In addition, Dr. Simpson warns:

There is a real need to alert parents and educators about the importance of protecting kids with Asperger's syndrome, placing them in situations where they are not going to be exposed to teasing and bullying classmates. Many times we feel too secure because these kids are high functioning, and we assume that they are going to be okay. These kids are extremely vulnerable and educators need to set up a supporting environment for them to be accepted as part of the student body.[63]

Because advances in the educational methods developed for autistic children have been so recent, many adults with Asperger's seek out services that will help them to catch up in learning social skills. In some communities, they can attend group sessions where facilitators use role playing, videos, games, team activities, and discussions to teach students the rules of the social world. Instructors address topics such as understanding autism, identifying and expressing emotions, learning conversational skills and body language, learning to communicate with friends and strangers (for instance, how to initiate contact, how close to stand, and how to end conversations), assertiveness, problem solving, how to behave in job interviews, and coping with stressful situations. In a study measuring the results of attending these classes, researchers reported that "all of the families reported improvements in [the autistic's] conversational and social skills, and in their appearance, self-confidence, and general independence."[64]

Many of the parents also reported that the group participants were getting better at making decisions, solving problems, and making and keeping friends. The participants themselves felt that meeting other people with similar problems had been extremely helpful. At the beginning of the year, almost all of the group members had lived at home and only two were employed. By the end of the year, some of the group members had moved to more independent living environments or gotten jobs.

## The Future for Adults with Asperger's

Researchers agree that children with Asperger's have a fairly good chance of functioning independently as adults, living on their own, holding jobs, dating, and even marrying. In fact, one group of researchers reported seeing eleven parents of autistic children who probably are mildly autistic themselves. Nine of the eleven were male, four of them had graduated with bachelor's degrees (one also had a law degree), and several had skilled jobs in fields such as computer programming and laboratory technology. These parents had problems similar to those of many adults with Asperger's, though less severe. Those who were employed seemed to have trouble keeping jobs, and all tended to be "loners," seemed insensitive, relied on rituals and compulsive behaviors such as lining up objects, spoke in monotone voices, and had problems relating to others.

These and other characteristics of life as an adult with Asperger's syndrome have been documented by Temple Grandin, an adult autistic woman who has written autobiographical

*In order for people with autism and Asperger's syndrome to succeed, it is crucial that they choose appropriate jobs by taking into account their own unique strengths and weaknesses.*

books and articles. Grandin completed her Ph.D. in animal science at the University of Illinois in Urbana and is now an assistant professor of animal science at Colorado State University. A well-known spokesperson for individuals with autism, she also has a successful international career designing livestock equipment.

Grandin has observed that many autistic adults who are talented and well educated fail to get and keep jobs that make use of their strengths. She explains:

> I was lucky to get headed on the right path after college. Three other high-functioning autistics were not so fortunate. One man has a Ph.D. in math and he sits at home. He needed somebody to steer him into an appropriate job. Teaching math did not work out; he should have obtained a research position that

*Temple Grandin demonstrates a prod that she designed to replace electric prods, which are stressful to cattle. Grandin, who is autistic, has achieved success as a professor, designer of livestock equipment, and spokesperson for autistics.*

required less interaction with people. The other lady has a degree in history and now works doing a boring telephone sales job. She needs a job where she can fully utilize her talents. She also needs a mentor to help her find an appropriate job and help open doors for her. Both these people needed support after college, and they did not receive it. The third man did well in high school and he also sits at home. He has a real knack for library research. If some interested person worked with him, he could work for a newspaper researching background information for stories. All three of these people need jobs where they can make maximum use of their talents and minimize their deficits.[65]

Grandin stresses the importance of choosing the right job based on the individual's abilities. For example, she recommends that visual thinkers with high-functioning autism or Asperger's go into fields like computer programming or repair, drafting, commercial art, photography, equipment design, automobile mechanics, small appliance repair, handcrafts, or building maintenance. She recommends that nonvisual thinkers with high-functioning autism or Asperger's (those who are good at math, music, or facts) go into accounting, library science, engineering, journalism, inventory control, or telemarketing.

Grandin also stresses the importance of finding a mentor who understands the autistic's weaknesses, someone who will coach the individual by pointing out inappropriate behavior. She still remembers getting hired for her first job at a large feedlot construction company.

The construction manager recognized my talents in design. He also served as a third important mentor to force me to conform to a few social rules. He had his secretaries take me out to buy better clothes. At the time I really resented this, but today I realize that he did me a great favor. He also told me bluntly that I had to do certain grooming niceties such as wearing deodorant. I had to change.[66]

For Temple Grandin and other autistics like her, meaningful work is important because the world of complex emotions and enriching friendships does not really exist. She says, "I put a great deal of emphasis on employment because I see so many very intelligent people with autism and Asperger's syndrome without satisfying jobs. A satisfying profession made life have meaning for me. I am what I do and think instead of what I feel."[67]

## Epilogue

# Future Research

A<small>UTISM AFFECTS MORE</small> than 400,000 U.S. families. In addition to the loss of personal potential, the cost of health and educational services to those affected is more than $13 billion a year. Despite the disorder's prevalence, autism research still receives less than 5 percent of the funding received by research into diseases that are far less common, such as multiple sclerosis and cystic fibrosis. Despite the great strides that have been made in understanding the disorder, researchers still seek answers to

*Unfortunately for families coping with autism, the causes for the disorder remain uncertain and there are no effective treatments or cure.*

fundamental questions about its causes, effective treatments or cure, prevention, and even accurate prevalence rates in the United States.

Three national autism advocacy organizations—the Autism Society of America (ASA), the National Alliance for Autism Research (NAAR), and Cure Autism Now (CAN)—work individually and together to lobby for legislation that will allocate additional funds for autism research. In the past, they have recommended spending money on studies that would determine how many children are newly diagnosed with autism and how many older children and adults suffer from the disorder. They have also sought funding to establish a center or interrelated centers that would be devoted to research in autism, attracting the country's top scientists and creating a system that would communicate the research findings to health professionals and the public. They have received legislative support in many areas and continue their efforts as research findings are reported and new areas for research are suggested.

Some new research focuses on identifying the gene or genes responsible for autism. The Collaborative Autism Project (CAP) has discovered areas on several chromosomes that may harbor autism genes, and it has received funding to continue to investigate those areas. The project is also studying families with two autistic children in order to compare their chromosomes and genetic material, while another study compares the genes of an autistic with a nonautistic sibling, which will allow the scientists to identify the genes that may be associated with autism.

On another front, research has shown that specific areas of the brain are responsible for specific activities. Different parts of the brain are activated, for example, when people read, tap their toes, listen to their favorite song, or think about what they had for dinner last night. A new technique called functional magnetic resonance imaging (fMRI) allows scientists to obtain "snapshots" of the brain while these areas are in use. CAP researchers will use the fMRI technology to study the brain activity in autistic adults while they are engaged in language tasks, comparing it with brain activity in nonautistic adults.

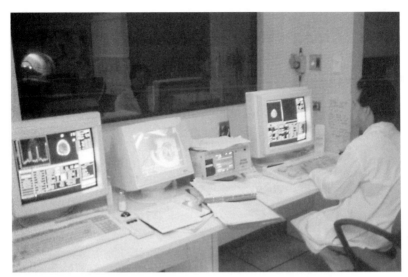

*A technician monitors the magnetic resonance imaging (MRI) scan of a patient's brain. Research that allows scientists to study brain activity in autistics may soon provide information needed to combat the disorder.*

Scientists may be very close to discovering how and why autism occurs, and perhaps how to prevent and cure it. In the meantime, medical experts advocate early detection as the key hope in ensuring access to necessary medical treatment and proper education. They stress that infants' routine doctor visits should be long enough that the physician can observe the baby's behavior, and recommend that doctors have specific written guidelines to help them spot developmental disabilities. Asking parents to fill out questionnaires about their children's behavior also helps doctors diagnose trouble early. "Early intervention would make all the difference in the world for a child with autism," says the mother of a child whose autism wasn't discovered until he was nearly five.

> We completely missed getting in on early intervention because our doctors didn't recognize it. It's a universal, national lament, that parents are having a difficult time getting their child diagnosed.[68]

In the meantime, the more the public understands people with autism, the greater the chances that the quality of autistics' lives will improve. Programs in schools that foster greater under-standing of the barriers faced by disabled people will ease the autistic's feelings of isolation and rejection. Employers who act as advocates and mentors for autistic adults in the workplace will find that these individuals may be able to contribute far more than earlier imagined. As autistics find that their skills, some of them quite remarkable, are of value to society, and that people are willing to accommodate their special needs, they are able to experience the satisfying sense of belonging that everyone seeks.

# Notes

## Introduction

1. Oliver Sacks, "Foreword," in *Thinking in Pictures*, by Temple Grandin. New York: Random House, 1995, pp. 11–12.

## Chapter 1: What Is Autism?

2. Quoted in Gary Mesibov, *Autism: Understanding the Disorder*. New York: Plenum Press, 1997, p. 5.
3. Quoted in Mesibov, *Autism*, p. 5.
4. National Institute of Mental Health (NIMH), "Autism," 1997. www.nimh.nih.gov/publicat/autism.cfm.
5. Autism Society of America. www.autism-society.org/autism.html.
6. NIMH, "Autism."
7. Laura Schreibman, *Autism*. Newbury Park, CA: Sage Publications, 1988, p. 43.
8. NIMH, "Autism."
9. NIMH, "Autism."
10. Quoted in Temple Grandin, *Thinking in Pictures*. New York: Random House, 1995, p. 76.
11. NIMH, "Autism."
12. Geoffrey Cowley, "Understanding Autism," *Newsweek*, July 31, 2000, pp. 49–50.
13. Clara Claiborne Park, *The Seige: The First Eight Years of an Autistic Child*. New York: Harcourt, Brace & World, 1967, p. 284.

## Chapter 2: Possible Causes and Treatments

14. Schreibman, *Autism*, p. 49.
15. Schreibman, *Autism*, p. 50.
16. Schreibman, *Autism*, p. 51.

17. "Autism Gene Link," *BBC News*, December 1, 1999. http://news6.thdo.bbc.co.uk/hi/english/health/newsid%5F544000/544055.stm.

18. Kelly Patricia O'Meara , "Inoculations May be Rx for Disaster," *Insight on the News*, October 4, 1999, p. 20.

19. Temple Grandin, "An Inside View of Autism," www.autism.org/temple/transition.html.

20. "Mother Stumbles Across Treatment for Autism," *BBC News*, September 14, 1998. http://news6.thdo.bbc.co.uk/hi/english/health/newsid%5F171000/171203.stm.

21. "Mother Stumbles Across Treatment for Autism."

22. Bernard Rimland, "Vitamin B6 (and Magnesium) in the Treatment of Autism," *Autism Research Review International*, no. 4 (1987).

23. Arthur Allen, "Why Are the Children Sick?" *Redbook*, November 1999, p. 150.

**Chapter 3: Options for Autistic Children**

24. Cowley, "Understanding Autism," p. 54.

25. "Train Parents to Help Autistic Children," *BBC News*, January 20, 2000. http://news6.thdo.bbc.co.uk/hi/english/health/newsid%5F611000/611666.stm.

26. "Autism: Learning to Understand Tom," *BBC News*, January 24, 2000. http://news6.thdo.bbc.co.uk/hi/english/health/newsid%5F617000/617134.stm.

27. "Autism: Learning to Understand Tom."

28. "Autism: Learning to Understand Tom."

29. "'Special Friends' Help Autistic Students Fit In," *Autism Research Review International*, 4, no. 1 (1990).

30. Quoted in Bernard Rimland, "'Full Inclusion': The Right Choice?" *Autism Research Review International*, 6, no. 4 (1992).

31. Quoted in Bernard Rimland, "Class Wars: Debate Intensifies Over 'Full Inclusion,'" *Autism Research Review International*, 7, no. 4 (1993).

32. Quoted in Rimland, "'Full Inclusion': The Right Choice?"

33. Quoted in Bernard Rimland, "Inclusive Education: Right for *Some*," *Autism Research Review International*, 7, no. 1 (1993).

34. Quoted in Rimland, "'Full Inclusion': The Right Choice?"
35. Quoted in Rimland, "'Full Inclusion': The Right Choice?"
36. Rimland, "Education Groups Charge That IDEA Endangers Regular Ed Teachers, Students," *Autism Research Review International*, 8, no. 4 (1995).
37. Quoted in Rimland, "Education Groups Charge That IDEA Endangers Regular Ed Teachers, Students."

### Chapter 4: Options for Autistic Adults

38. Autism-PDD Resource Network, "Getting Ready for College: Advising High School Students with Disabilities." www.autism-pdd.net.
39. Temple Grandin, "Making the Transition from the World of School to the World of Work." www.autism.org/temple/inside.html.
40. Interview with Transitional Program Director at the Stein Education Center, San Diego, California, July 2000.
41. Bernard Rimland, "The Non-Urban Alternative," *Autism Research Review International*, 4, no. 3 (1990).
42. Quoted in Rimland, "The Non-Urban Alternative."
43. Quoted in Rimland, "The Non-Urban Alternative."

### Chapter 5: The Autistic Savant and Asperger's Syndrome

44. Bernard Rimland, "Savant Capabilities of Autistic Children and Their Cognitive Implications," in *Cognitive Defects in the Development of Mental Illness*, edited by George Serban. New York: Brunner/Mazel, 1978, p. 44.
45. Bernard Rimland, "Inside the Mind of the Autistic Savant," *Psychology Today*, August 1978.
46. Bernard Rimland, "*Rain Man* and the Savants' Secrets," *Autism Research Review International*, 3, no. 1 (1989).
47. Alison Blake, "Real 'Rain Men': The Mystery of the Savant," *Autism Research Review International*, 3, no. 1 (1989).
48. Lawrence Osborne, "The Little Professor Syndrome," *New York Times Magazine*, June 18, 2000, p. 56.
49. Bernard Rimland and A. Lewis Hill, "Idiot Savants," in *Mental Retardation and Developmental Disabilities*, vol. 13, edited by Joseph Wortis. New York: Plenum Press, 1984, pp. 156–57.

50. Rimland and Hill, "Idiot Savants," p. 157.

51. Rimland and Hill, "Idiot Savants," p. 158.

52. Bernard Rimland and Deborah Fein, "Special Talents of Autistic Savants," in *The Exceptional Brain*, edited by Lorraine K. Obler and Deborah Fein. New York: Buildford Press, 1988, pp. 475–76.

53. Rimland, "*Rain Man* and the Savants' Secrets."

54. Rimland, "*Rain Man* and the Savants' Secrets."

55. Rimland, "*Rain Man* and the Savants' Secrets."

56. Rimland, "*Rain Man* and the Savants' Secrets."

57. Osborne, "The Little Professor Syndrome," pp. 56–57.

58. Quoted in Alison Blake, "Asperger's Syndrome: Is It Autism?" *Autism Research Review International*, 2, no. 4 (1988).

59. Quoted in Blake, "Asperger's Syndrome: Is It Autism?"

60. Osborne, "The Little Professor Syndrome," p. 56.

61. Osborne, "The Little Professor Syndrome," p. 59.

62. Richard L. Simpson, interviewed by Dr. Stephen M. Edelson, November 23, 1998, www.autism.org.

63. Simpson interview.

64. Bernard Rimland, "Social Skills Training: Praise for Benefits, but 'Don't Raise False Hopes,'" *Autism Research Review International UPDATE*, 13, nos. 1–4 (1999).

65. Grandin, "An Inside View of Autism."

66. Grandin, "Making the Transition from the World of School into the World of Work."

67. Temple Grandin, "Social Problems: Understanding Emotions and Developing Talents." www.autism.org/temple/social.html.

**Epilogue: Future Research**

68. Teri Sforza, "UCI Expect Improving Diagnosis of Autism: Doctors Are to Spend More Time with Infants to Recognize Symptoms," *Orange County Register*, January 5, 2000.

# Organizations to Contact

**Autism Research Institute**
4182 Adams Avenue
San Diego, CA 92116
(619) 281-7165
(619) 563-6840
Internet: www.autism.com/ari

This organization conducts research on autism and makes it available to the families of autistics and the general public. Has extensive library of books, information pamphlets, audiocassettes, and videotapes on all aspects of autism.

**Autism Society of America**
7910 Woodmont Avenue, Suite 300
Bethesda, MD 20814-3015
(800)-3AUTISM, ext. 150
Internet: www.autism-society.org

This organization increases public awareness about the day-to-day issues faced by individuals with autism, their families, and the professionals with whom they interact. They provide information and education, supporting research and advocating for programs and services for the autism population.

**CAN, The Cure Autism Now Foundation**
5225 Wilshire Boulevard, Suite 226
Los Angeles, CA 90036
(888) 8AUTISM
email: info@cureautismnow.org
Internet: www.canfoundation.org

This organization raises funds to support research to find effective treatments, prevention, and a cure for autism and related disorders.

**Center for the Study of Autism**
P.O. Box 4538
Salem, OR 97302
Internet: www.autism.com

This organization provides information about autism to parents and professionals and conducts research on the effectiveness of existing treatments. Much of their research is done in collaboration with the Autism Research Institute.

# For Further Reading

**Books**

Temple Grandin, *Thinking in Pictures*, Foreword by Oliver Sacks. New York: Random House, 1995. An inspiring account of one woman's experience with autism, from her earliest memories to her experience in the academic world and as a well-respected professional.

Charles Hart, *Without Reason: A Family Copes with Two Generations of Autism*. New York: Harper & Row, 1989. A sensitive and perceptive account of a family's struggles and unique ways of coping with autistic children.

Clara Claiborne Park, *The Siege: The First Eight Years of an Autistic Child*. New York: Harcourt, Brace & World, 1967. The mother of an autistic daughter shares her experiences and gives hope to other families of autistic children.

Donna Williams, *Nobody Nowhere: The Extraordinary Autobiography of an Autistic*. New York: Random House, 1992. Once labeled deaf, retarded, disturbed, and insane, Williams has written an insightful memoir, recounting her struggle with the disorder.

**Periodicals**

Geoffrey Cowley, "Understanding Autism," *Newsweek*, July 31, 2000.

Lawrence Osborne, "The Little Professor Syndrome," *New York Times Magazine*, June 18, 2000.

Oliver Sacks, "An Anthropologist on Mars," *New Yorker*, December 27, 1994.

# Works Consulted

## Books

Gary Mesibov, *Autism: Understanding the Disorder*. New York: Plenum Press, 1997. A collection of scientific research articles about the diagnosis, causes, and treatment of autism.

Bernard Rimland and Deborah Fein, "Special Talents of Autistic Savants," in *The Exceptional Brain*, edited by Lorraine K. Obler and Deborah Fein. New York: Buildford Press, 1988.

Bernard Rimland and A. Lewis Hill, "Idiot Savants," in *Mental Retardation and Developmental Disabilities*, vol. 13, edited by Joseph Wortis. New York: Plenum Press, 1984.

Bernard Rimland, "Savant Capabilities of Autistic Children and Their Cognitive Implications," *Cognitive Defects in the Development of Mental Illness*, edited by George Serban. New York: Brunner/Mazel, 1978.

Michael Rutter and Eric Schopler, eds., *Autism: A Reappraisal of Concepts and Treatment*. New York: Plenum Press, 1979. Contributors report on research conducted and evaluate new ideas and concepts for treating autism.

Laura Schreibman, *Autism*. Newbury Park, CA: Sage Publications, 1988. For professionals in the field, a review of autism's history, diagnosis, causes, and treatments.

## Periodicals

Arthur Allen, "Why Are the Children Sick?," *Redbook*, November 1999.

Alison Blake, "Asperger's Syndrome: Is It Autism?" *Autism Research Review International*, 2, no. 4 (1988).

_____, "Real 'Rain Men': The Mystery of the Savant," *Autism Research Review International*, 3, no. 1 (1989).

Kelly Patricia O'Meara, "Inoculations May be Rx for Disaster," *Insight on the News*, October 4, 1999.

Bernard Rimland, "Class Wars: Debate Intensifies Over 'Full Inclusion,'" *Autism Research Review International*, 7, no. 4 (1993).

———, "Education Groups Charge That IDEA Endangers Regular Ed Teachers, Students," *Autism Research Review International*, 8, no. 4 (1995).

———, "'Full Inclusion': The Right Choice?" *Autism Research Review International*, 6, no. 4 (1992).

———, "Inclusive Education: Right for *Some*," *Autism Research Review International*, 7, no. 1 (1993).

———, "Inside the Mind of the Autistic Savant," *Psychology Today*, August 1978.

———, "The Non-Urban Alternative," *Autism Research Review International*, 4, no. 3 (1990).

———, "*Rain Man* and the Savants' Secrets," *Autism Research Review International*, 3, no. 1 (1989).

———, "Social Skills Training: Praise for Benefits, but 'Don't Raise False Hopes,'" *Autism Research Review International UPDATE*, 13, nos. 1–4 (1999).

———, "Vitamin $B_6$ (and Magnesium) in the Treatment of Autism," *Autism Research Review International*, 1, no. 4 (1987).

Teri Sforza, "UCI Expect Improving Diagnosis of Autism: Doctors Are to Spend More Time with Infants to Recognize Symptoms," *Orange County Register*, January 5, 2000.

"'Special Friends' Help Autistic Students Fit In," *Autism Research Review International*, 4, no. 1 (1990).

**Internet Sources**

"Autism Gene Link," *BBC News*, December 1, 1999. http://news6.thdo.bbc.co.uk/hi/english/health/newsid%5F544000/544055.stm.

"Autism: Learning to Understand Tom," *BBC News*, January 24, 2000. http://news6.thdo.bbc.co.uk/hi/english/health/newsid%5F617000/617134.stm.

Autism-PDD Resource Network, "Getting Ready for College:

Advising High School Students with Disabilities." www. autism-pdd.net.

Temple Grandin, "An Inside View of Autism." www.autism. org/temple/inside.html.

————, "Making the Transition from the World of School to the World of Work." www.autism.org/temple/transition.html.

————, "Social Problems: Understanding Emotions and Developing Talents." www.autism.org/temple/social.html.

"Mother Stumbles Across Treatment for Autism," *BBC News*, September 14, 1998. http://news6.thdo.bbc.co.uk/hi/english/health/newsid%5F171000/171203.stm.

National Institute of Mental Health (NIMH), "Autism," 1997. www.nimh.nih.gov/publicat/autism.cfm.

Richard L. Simpson, interviewed by Dr. Stephen M. Edelson, November 23, 1998. www.autism.org.

"Train Parents to Help Autistic Children," *BBC News*, January 20, 2000. http://news6.thdo.bbc.co.uk/hi/english/health/news id%5F611000/611666.stm.

**Website**

Autism Society of America (www.autism-society.org)

**Interviews**

Interview with Transitional Program Director at the Stein Education Center, San Diego, California, July 2000.

# Index

# *Picture Credits*

## About the Author

Michele Engel Edwards earned a bachelor's degree with honors in education from the University of New Mexico, where she majored in English and minored in social studies. She has worked for one of the largest national volunteer health organizations in the United States and managed clinical trials for a major university. Her career has also included writing promotional materials for major corporations and publishing magazine articles. She lives with her husband in San Diego, California.